Six Men on the Stour

ERNEST J. BRETT

First published 1985.

Original manuscript copyright © the estate of E. J. Brett 1985.
Published edition copyright © William T. Topp 1985.
Introduction and biographical notes copyright © Roger Guttridge 1985.

All rights reserved. No part of this publication may be reproduced, stored in a retrieval system, or transmitted, in any form or by any means, electronic, mechanical, photocopying, recording or otherwise, without the prior permission of the publishers.

Cover design by Peter Goad. Map by Sylvia Guttridge.
Photographic copying by Bob Richardson.

Typeset by SOS Typesetters, Bell Street, Shaftesbury, Dorset.
Printed by Wincanton Litho at the Old National School, North Street, Wincanton, Somerset.
Published by Roger Guttridge and William T. Topp from
7 Greenhill Close, Colehill, Wimborne, Dorset, BH21 2RQ. (Tel: 0202-886289)

ISBN 0 948678 00 3

INTRODUCTION

Boating was a popular pastime in the late Victorian era, all the more so following the publication in 1889 of Jerome K. Jerome's classic of British humour Three Men in a Boat. The book, describing the antics of three men and a dog on the River Thames, was an instant success and probably inspired many a young man – and woman – to take to the water with oar and sail. Whether it also inspired the Stour Expedition of 1892 we can only speculate but the similarities of the situation are striking.

It was just after 7 a.m. on Monday 18 July 1892 when two sturdy boats put off from a river bank at Wimborne Minster, Dorset, and an epic journey got underway. On board were five young men with a thirst for adventure and a cargo sufficient to keep them fed and sheltered for more than a week. The Stour Expedition, as it was grandly entitled, had been a year in the planning and had been the main topic of conversation among its intended participants for weeks. The plan was to explore the lower reaches of the River Stour, from Wimborne downstream to the sea at Mudeford, Hampshire (now Dorset), camping along the route and partaking of whatever experiences and adventures might come their way.

The expedition lasted nine days – including five at the group's so called "permanent camp" on Avon Beach, Mudeford – and contained no shortage of incident. There were encounters – some amicable and some less so – with gamekeepers and millers, with fishermen and coastguards, with simpletons and drinkers, with the local lads and lasses. For six young men from Victorian Wimborne (five set out but six came back!), it was the holiday of a lifetime with memories to last them a lifetime.

Lest, however, the memories should fade, one of the crew, Ernest "the Skipper" Brett, was urged to make a written record of the expedition.

"It being the wish expressed by you that some little account of our pleasant holiday last summer should be chronicled," he wrote, "I have applied myself to the task. How far I have succeeded is only too apparent; I confess myself it is anything but what I would wish."

Skipper Brett, as he was known for most of his life, succeeded, in my view, rather well. He was not a literary master like Jerome K. Jerome and did not aspire to such heights. (Indeed, he concludes the account with a modest postscript stating that "I don't pretend to be a writer or historian and my advice to anyone who reads it and doesn't like it is to do the other thing. It isn't wanted to be liked.") But by most people's standards he was no mean quill-driver and his 20,000-word tongue-in-cheek description is full of colour and humour and conveys the full flavour of Victorian life.

Skipper Brett wrote his manuscript by hand and illustrated it with a small number of his own pen and ink drawings in the margins, a printed map with the route of the expedition marked out in red ink and 11 photographs taken during the holiday. Then he had the whole work bound in a leather case (hard cover) measuring 13¼ inches (33½ centimetres) by nine inches (22½ centimetres).

The document's preservation is due largely to retired Wimborne ironmonger Mr Bill Topp, a former chairman of Wimborne Minster Urban District Council, who has collected old photographs and memorabilia of Wimborne for much of his life. At some time in the 1930s or 40s, Frank Kerridge, son of one of the members of the Stour Expedition, gave him what is now the only known copy of the original manuscript as an addition to his collection. Mr Topp kept the document in a cupboard for half-a-century and rediscovered it in 1983 while preparing to move out of his bungalow in Gravel Hill, Merley. He invited me, as a local journalist, to read it and it was from this conversation that our decision to publish the book emerged.

In this, the first published edition, Skipper Brett's account of the expedition is reproduced verbatim save for corrections to the author's errors of spelling and punctuation. Any grammatical errors or "invented" words (such as "ridiculosity"!) have been allowed to remain. A small number of explanatory notes have been included in square brackets and the Skipper's sketches and photographs taken by the crew have been supplemented by other photographs from a variety of sources.

Brief biographical notes on the six members of the expedition appear on another page. It has not so far been possible to identify with certainty any of the supporting characters in the book, although publication of it could produce new information, as could the publication in 1992 of the 1891 national census. Tucker, a young Christchurch man who became friendly with the Wimborne crew during their stay at Mudeford, may have been connected with the family who kept the general store of W. Tucker and Son in the High Street from 1798. The man who owned the business at the time of the expedition, William Tucker, was Mayor of Christchurch five times between 1891 and 1918.

It has also not been possible to indentify positively the big house near the shore at Mudeford, from which the crew drew some of their more essential supplies, including food, water and female companionship (though of the last, sadly, there was insufficient to go round!). It was certainly in the vicinity of Avon Beach and the favourite candidate, I think, is the large red brick house called Capesthorne which was until recent years used as a children's home but was due for demolition and redevelopment at the time of publication.

ROGER GUTTRIDGE
WIMBORNE, 1985.

ACKNOWLEDGMENTS

The publishers are particularly grateful to Mrs Aphra Brett, daughter-in-law of Skipper Brett, for her co-operation and for the loan of the portrait photograph of him taken in 1917. They also wish to thank Bob Richardson and Phil Yeomans for photographic work and the following for permission to reproduce photographs: Allen White (three pictures of Mudeford, two of Iford and one of Heron Court); Alan Dean (Longham cottages); the Priest's House Museum, Wimborne (Canford Mill, Dudsbury c. 1912, Arthur Kerridge and his shop and two pictures of Canford suspension bridge); Hampshire County Council Museums Service (Throop Mill c. 1900).

MEMBERS OF THE STOUR EXPEDITION 1892

ERNEST JOHN BRETT, known as "the Skipper", was born in the Dorchester area in 1872. He trained as an architect under Walter Fletcher and George Evans of Wimborne and was later a partner of the firm Fletcher, Son and Brett. He designed many prominent buildings in the Wimborne area and also became architect to the Dorset Education Committee. He lived in West Borough and later Highland Road and married Emily Blanche Keen of Chewton Mendip at Victoria Falls, Rhodesia (now Zimbabwe), in 1904. He had two sons, Leonard, an actor and television producer (he produced the ITV serial Emergency Ward 10), who died circa 1959, and Reynolds Brett (1908-81), who succeeded his father as an architect in Wimborne. Skipper Brett died in 1940 and his ashes were scattered at Win Green, near Shaftesbury, his favourite beauty spot.

WILLIAM DARKE D. BRETT, known as "Bill" or "Will", was a brother of Skipper Brett and was born in the Dorchester area in 1870. At the time of the Stour Expedition, he appears to have been living in South Wales. A third brother, Leonard, was apprenticed to Addis the Chemist of Wimborne but died of typhoid as a young man. Skipper Brett's daughter-in-law, Mrs. Aphra Brett, says one brother – possibly Thomas – is supposed to have "walked off with a Bible and gone to Canada!"

MURRAY MARSH KERRIDGE, known as "the Admiral", was born at Wimborne in 1867, son of Benjamin and Jane Kerridge. He followed his father's trade as a watchmaker and jeweller and kept shops at various times in West Borough, High Street and East Street, Wimborne. He married at Wimborne Minster in 1896. Bill Topp recalls that he was about five feet 11 inches tall and was the father of Frank and Jack Kerridge.

ARTHUR JOHN KERRIDGE, known as "the Big Un" or "the Long Un", was a brother of Murray Kerridge and was born at Wimborne in 1869. He was an antique furniture dealer with a shop in the High Street. Bill Topp recalls that he was a very tall man – about six feet three inches – hence his nickname, presumably.

Arthur Kerridge outside his shop in Wimborne High Street.

JAMES ELLIS JENVEY, known as "Jimbly", was born at Wimborne in 1871, son of James Ellis Jenvey and Selina Jenvey. His father is variously described as an accountant, auctioneer, valuer, land agent, assessor of taxes for Wimborne, secretary to Wimborne Conservative Club and member of Wimborne Urban District Council. Mr Topp believes that Jimbly himself ran a dairy in East Street and was killed in the first world war but no documentary confirmation of these statements has been found so far.

ARTHUR WILTON KELLAWAY, may be the same man as the "Wilkie" Kellaway of the Stour Expedition but this is unproven. Arthur Wilton Kellaway (born 1865) was certainly the only Kellaway whose birth was registered at Wimborne between 1862 and 1874 and the Minster baptismal register for 1865 shows him to be the son of Arthur and Maria Kellaway of Wool, with father's occupation recorded as "labourer". Bill Topp thinks Wilkie Kellaway was a farmer who lived in The Avenue (otherwise Avenue Road), Wimborne. Kelly's Directories of Dorsetshire for 1903 and 1911 list a Thomas Kellaway in Avenue Road but no Wilkie or Arthur Wilton Kellaway.

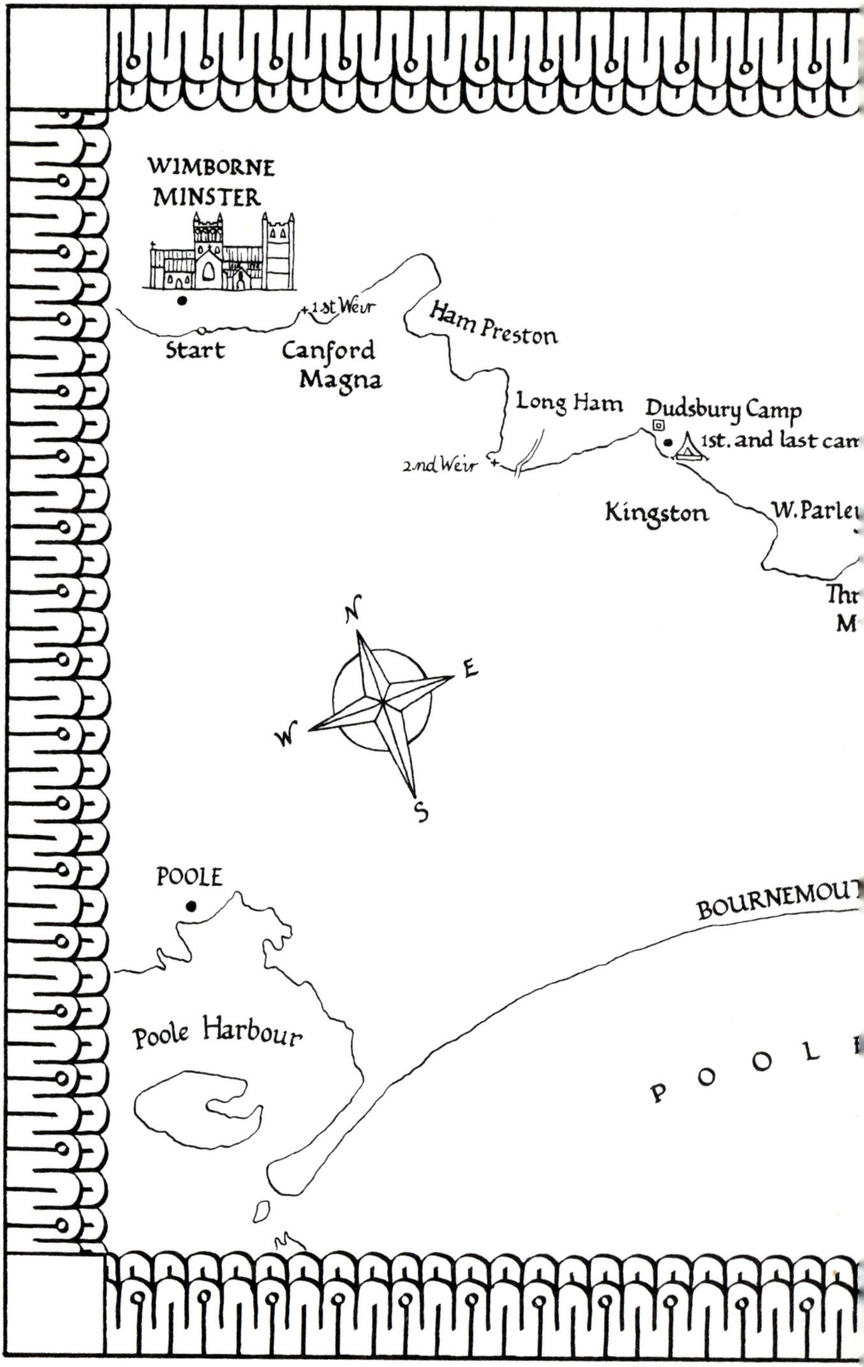

WIMBORNE MINSTER
1st Weir
Start
Canford Magna
Ham Preston
Long Ham
Dudsbury Camp
1st. and last cam
2nd Weir
Kingston
W. Parle
N
E
W
S
POOLE
BOURNEMOUT
Poole Harbour
P O O L

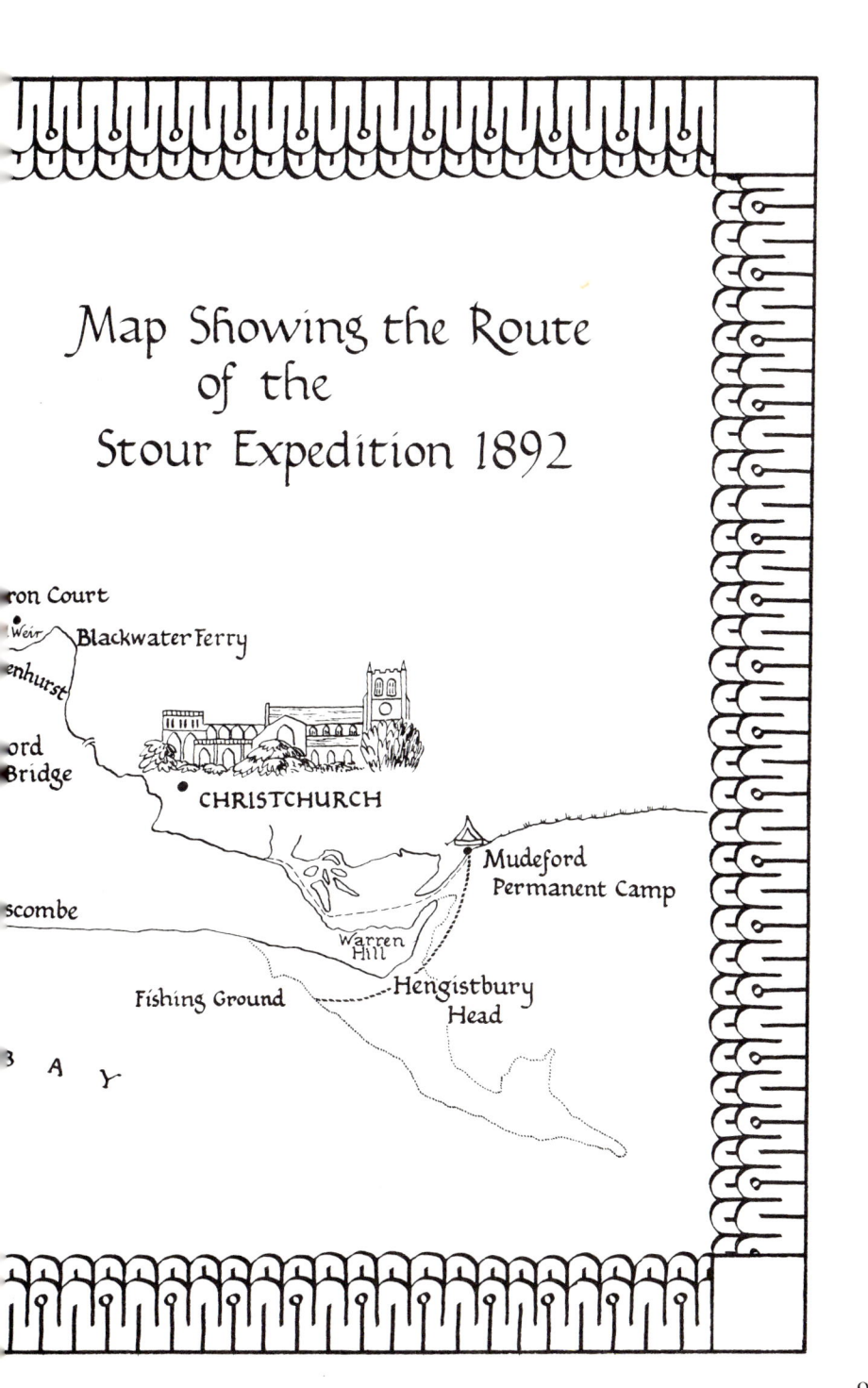

Map Showing the Route of the Stour Expedition 1892

The Skipper's original title page, with "holiday" mis-spelt.

To members of the Stour Expedition, July 1892.

Dear Companions,

It being the wish expressed by you that some little account of our pleasant holiday last summer should be chronicled, I have applied myself to the task. How far I have succeeded is only too apparent; I confess myself it is anything but what I would wish. There is an alternative, however, which will obviate everything: Don't read it!

If there is anything written which will cause offence, I crave your pardon: it is done unwittingly and as such I hope you will forgive me.

In fancy sometimes I see a grey-headed, gouty, crippled old man hobbling across the room; he stretches out his strengthless arm and takes up a volume; with great difficulty he makes out the scrawl of bygone days, and yet like other books, he does not give it up, but reads patiently on; his thoughts wander back to the merry days of youth, he calls to mind the kind companions, alas! many now gone. The old, badly-written volume does its work; he remembers there was such a place as Mudeford and such a girl as Nellie.

Yours sincerely,
Skipper Ernest Brett
Wimborne Minster
March 1893.

Skipper Brett in 1917.

THE STOUR EXPEDITION 1892

Where we went, how we went, what we did and what we didn't, told by The Skipper.

Yes! We had discussed and thought of the scheme last year and now another year had come and was advancing to the middle of summer.
"We'll go, Skipper, if we go by ourselves!"
"Of course we'll go," said I. "You don't think I did all that scraping, tarring and painting, spoilt my clothes and injured my health for nothing? Oh, no! We'll go!"
"Do you think the other fellows will go?"
"Of course. Jimbly's game, my brother and Kelly, to a certainty. Brown I don't count on, there's no certainty with him."
"Well, I vote we begin to see about it and settle who's going and who's not."
"Yes, certainly. Tell Jimbly to come down tomorrow and we'll talk it over."
"All right. By jove, it's half-past two. I'm off."

Somehow, I don't know how it is, but the time seems to go so quickly out from business, and drag along in the office so slow, that we have to contrive some innocent amusement at times to help it a bit. I've known ten minutes seem an hour. Sometimes, only very occasionally, we close round the fire place in the office ten minutes before time and begin some argument. We're a regular argumentative lot in our office. Sometimes we get warm. I remember I unfolded our scheme to my fellow confidants who, of course, not being able to go, declared the expedition impossible. (I should have done precisely the same if I wasn't going.) That riled me. I laid down in my best and most forcible language the ridiculosity of the assertion, standing on tiptoe to look as important as possible. (I'm obliged to do that sometimes, and even then five feet three inches doesn't seem to tell; then they smile gently at me, and look over me with a beaming face and smile one to another; it's maddening and cruel but there's no remedy.)

Well! I was just warm on the subject when the door opened and in walked the governor. There was a general rush. Somebody knocked over a chair. I grasped a letter and was intently reading when the cheery(?) voice of the Gov. exclaimed: "Can you read upside down, Brett?"

The Stour at Wimborne. Photo by Skipper Brett.

I put the letter down. "Hang the expedition," I muttered when the chief had departed. It always happens, of course. Must be me. "Why will you fellows make me talk?"

"Why, it's you," they warmly exclaim. "You began it."

So I did. Vowing I would never discuss it again, I went out.

Three of us met next day at our usual meeting place, which is a branch business of one of our number. It's not a large place – it consists of a shop and a workshop. Never in the memory of any of us has work been known to have been done in that workshop; perhaps we never call at the right time?

The first thing that strikes one on entering it is the peculiar aroma; not pleasant the first thing in the morning but to be tolerated more as the day advances. Many a time we have had to feel for the means of exit, so dense is the atmosphere. Even when the gas is lit the place is generally like a London fog. The cause is the detestable liking of the inmates and callers for that vulgar weed tobacco. The place reeks of it. Even the walls begin to show signs of distress and the bench is quite discoloured. If only the amount of money so squandered in smoke had been given to the missionaries, China by this time would have been a Christian country and opium smoking known no more. But it is otherwise. Why, we know not.

"Well, how goes it now?" (We generally say that.) "Where's yer pipe? Just a toothful."

So I pull out my briar and more smoke. I'm accommodated with a box to sit on and then we fall to.

"Well, when do you think of starting?" says Jimbly.

"Let's know who's going first," says I.

"We want the date first," says he.

"What's the use of a date if you don't know who's going?"

"What's the use of knowing who's going if you don't know when?"

At last it's decided that it shall be who's going and I'm ruled out once more.

"I'm one, I started the idea," says the Admiral (self-dubbed). The Admiral is the third of four brothers known principally for their extreme piety.

"You put 'em down, Skipper." So I do as I'm told (I've generally got to) and head the list with Kerridge, Murray.

"Well, there's my brother, Arthur," so down goes ditto Arthur. "Then there's your brother – you say he's going?"

"Of course," says I, and down goes Brett, William.

"And me," says Jimbly.

"Right," say I. "Down with Jenvey, James," (since known as Jimbly). "Brown won't go but Wilkie will," and down goes Kellaway, Wilkie. "That's five."

"No, it's not. It's six."

"Five," say I.

"You fool, you can't count."

"Well ..." I read out the list.

"You haven't put yourself down, you ass. Upon my word you have got a head."

So I meekly put down Brett, E., commonly known as the Skipper, probably so called because he has the least authority in his own tub. He owns a tub, but of that later on.

It's arranged! They all consented to go. Members might be seen hanging up talking at the corners of streets, club doors, church doors; it was always the expedition, everything was on that subject. Sometimes I caught myself murmuring the word. I've even sat in my chair at the office, oblivious of everything, and then the fellows would whisper

Will Brett (left) and his wife and brother Leonard. Photo by Skipper Brett.

"Expedition", and so it was. I verily believe, if the affair had not come off when it did, I should have made an expedition of rather a different kind to the west of the county.

Visions of the expedition were seen in my sleep and in my daydreams, too. However, the time went by until the list of necessaries had to be written out, ordered and afterwards paid for (I'm rather afraid it was afterwards). But stop! I've forgotten to tell you, Reader, what the expedition was. Lucky I've not got the eye of one of the crew on me or ... well, I won't say what.

The idea was to get to Mudeford, which is situate on the coast of the English Channel just beyond the town of Christchurch, Hampshire, by boats, following the River Stour to its mouth from the town of Wimborne Minster, camping out under canvas the whole of the time.

A vast idea, gentlemen! Nothing but a brain of extraordinary calibre could e'er have suggested such a heavy undertaking. And a very heavy undertaking it was!

The first thing was a tent, and the question: should we hire or buy one? From advertisements, an old army tent can be purchased for the modest sum of 18/6d. We enquired the hire of one and found it would be 10 shillings per week and carriage both ways, a matter of 15 shillings,

The Iolanthe ... from Skipper Brett's photograph album.

say. After a heated discussion, it was decided to hire, as the result of purchasing one would lead, no doubt, to disastrous results. The point which decided it was similar to the well-known question, "Which man's wife would she be?" Or to whom would the tent belong?

When the tent business was started, the members of the expedition had something tangible to work at. The agent who was to supply the canvas was badgered at every corner. Always the tent. The way that poor man was assailed was awful, but he would have been killed outright if we could have foreseen what a tent it would be.

I met Jimbly one morning. With a terrible yell and a dash from the opposite side of the street, he pounced upon me. Says he: "Have you heard the news?"

"What news?"

"You mean to say you've not heard?" and his face turned perfectly livid as he gasped out: "Wilkie isn't going."

You could have knocked me down with a feather. To think, after the many nights he had discussed the enjoyable evenings we were to have; what good cheer he would bring us; what large cigars. All these things flitted through my mind (and a great deal more). Seeing what a terrible blow he had dealt me, Jimbly led me quietly away. We discussed how mean it was of him just as the last to throw up. Going to Paris was his

plea. I rather wish he'd gone and then perhaps he would have remembered Tom Hood's lines:
> *Don't go to France without you know the lingo;*
> *If you do, by chance, you will repent, by Jingo,*

an example of which we have just had, and I don't think the gentleman will try it again.

I met the Admiral one morning.

"Here, Skipper, the time's going on. We start next Monday and today's Tuesday. No list of stores yet got out. We shall find ourselves in the wrong box brinly." (Brinly is a substitute for by and by with that gent.)

"Well, what can I do?"

"Do? Why, come down and see me lunch time instead of wandering off in the idiotic manner you do. Come down this afternoon. Jimbly's coming."

I went down. After a good deal of tobacco, the list was prepared. There was ox tongue, beef and every variety of tinned stuff; also tinned fruit, potted chicken, ham, etc. I suggested jam – that was cried down as suitable for children only. Now if there's one thing I like, it's jam. I had pictured and fancied myself sitting in the sun and eating jam until my mouth watered with expectation. I'd fancied I would take every sort of jam – strawberry, apricot, gooseberry and plum. What rich variety! And I would have the finest and best whole fruit jam. What a feed I would

"Under Merley." Photo by Skipper Brett.

have! And when the others were away, I'd stow jam. So I stuck up and would not give in; and so resolutely did I dilate on the necessity of jam that they allowed one pot. One pot only! Just to quiet me. As long as they consented, I was all right, so I gave way to everything they fancied, especially one gentleman (sardines). We completed the list at last and I was deputed to order them from the grocer. When I got that list, how I amended it: it took quite one whole afternoon. I added four pots and marked "large" by the side. I also added a few more things I have rather a weakness for.

Jimbly was deputed for cooking utensils etc., among which were the following – spirit stove, kettle, frying pan, enamelled cups, bowls and plates. Each was to bring a knife, fork and spoon. The Admiral took the wine and spirit branch (he naturally would).

Oh! how the days went by. I called at the grocer's to know how the order was getting on every day. At last it was Friday morning and Jimbly and I, according to arrangement, got up punctually at 6 a.m. and armed with mops, monkey-hands and other cleansing manufactures, made for our tub. It was cold to off boots and socks and we stepped gingerly into the water. We did clean her, too; turned her up and scrubbed every board in her, and she looked tolerably clean when we left. But to Jimbly's eye she wanted just a little varnish, so in the evening he journeyed forth with varnish and brush, and in the twilight the gunwale was varnished. The result, when we looked at her Sunday (we generally look at her that day) was a gunwale all shinily white, bristling all over with white hair. I sat on it, too, Sunday, on Jimbly's assurance that it would be perfectly dry. It held me fast; however, with the united efforts of myself and brother, I got off, but left part of my habiliments behind.

The excitement was now getting to a terrible pitch. My brother had already arrived from South Wales and everything was ready. Saturday was a busy day – everybody was running one over the other. The stores and tent were at Jimbly's awaiting shipment.

We adjourned to the club after the day's work, as usual, for a quiet game of billiards. I remember I was making a tremendous break (my breaks generally are) when, oh, such a yell! and the door suddenly opened and Jimbly fell headlong on the floor. We took him up in a perfect dead faint; his face was fearful in the extreme.

We roused him with muffins,
We roused him with ice,
We roused him with mustard and cress ...

and when brought to, he was faintly heard to murmur: "Bread, the staff of life."

"Yes," one replied., "Certainly."

No-one could make out what he meant and we thought the excitement had turned his brain. Someone ventured to suggest it. That remark saved him, and the fainted one slowly explained that no bread had been provided and, perfectly true, it had been forgotten. Saved! Just saved! And in thankfulness, we deputed him to secure a supply, which he did, and two foot of cake in the bargain.

Sunday morning at last! This is the last morning I shall sleep in this stuffy bed, I thought to myself; no more being pent up for fresh air; ozone in plenty and don't pay for it, either. But it was rather a damper on looking out – the rain was coming down in bucketsfull and clouds looking full of it, as rough as a wild March morning. Too late to go to church, and not inclined for it either, so I fell to with Bill (i.e. my respected brother) discussing the situation, and it needed a good deal of cussing (beg pardon, I mean dis-cussing) to bring oneself to resignation. To think, for a whole month, every day fine weather and just on starting it should be like this. It was mortifying. One couldn't stay in and endure it so out we went. With Jimbly, of course. He called. All tried to look unconcerned about it, but from the corkscrew sighs it was a failure. Of course, everyone swore that he didn't mind, in fact rather expected it.

Our footsteps naturally wandered up by the river and our speech was sad and slow. Coming along we were surprised to see another of the

Canford Bridge, Wimborne.

Starting point... the Stour at Wimborne, c. 1892. The man's identity is unknown. Photo by Skipper Brett.

crew. His long form was keeping up a willow tree in a very graceful fashion. We approached him gently and saw his face was sad and, as he looked into the waters, could understand the tear in his dimmed eye. He too thought of the morrow and what it might have been: visions of a blue sky and gentle breeze, softly stirring the waters of a winding river; and boats with sails set, sailing pleasantly along; with happy mortals basking in the sunshine; and at the stern of one, a form much larger than the rest appeared, whose face was beaming with contentment; and by his side there was a vessel, marked double X; and near, a glass half-full, from which he, time to time, did quaff and fill again at pleasure.

At last, he aroused himself from his reverie, and gently wiped the teardrops from his eye; strode sorrowfully away.

Troubles like these are ones that make life sad, hopes blighted and expectations blasted. Why they are sent into this world we know not, but that they do come we are assured.

"Oh! hullo! Nice weather."

"Isn't it?" we exclaim.

"What can you expect in this hole of a country," is the reply. "Chuck the lot, it's no use thinking of going. Even if it does clear up, it would simply mean rheumatic fever or something of the kind."

So, in the "more in sorrow than in anger" style, we wend home.

The weather, by some unaccountable means, changed in the afternoon and the evening was tolerably fine, so it was arranged to start at 6 a.m. on the morrow.

At last, the eventful morning, July 18th A.D. 1892, broke: a cloudy, gloomy morning. Having been dilatory in getting up, we (i.e. my brother and I) were late. Hearty indeed was the greeting as we caught sight of the other fellows and the hangers-on with trucks containing the provisions etc.

At least one might call it warm. However, the fact of starting calmed the ruffled ones. The boats were unmoored and moored to the side of the banks. The amount of luggage was considerable – it put one in mind of a travelling theatrical company. Willing hands, however, soon stowed it away and all was ready. It was agreed that the heavier boat (or tub, as sometimes called, but nevertheless a good tub, perhaps a trifle heavy) should tow the lighter into which was stowed most of the cargo.

It was a proud moment for every one of the crew as the boats got under way at a few minutes past seven. They felt their hearts beat with a glow of satisfaction as a few early risers on the bridge waved their hands adieu, and owner of the land, our county councillor, bid us God speed.

The Admiral addressed a few words to the crew, telling of the great unknown to be traversed and the glory of succeeding; but I'm sorry the thought of those left behind piped his eye (and another one's, too) and soon after he eyed his pipe.

Canford Manor, home of Lord Wimborne, c. 1903.

We dropped downstream gently. Soon the suspension bridge appeared in sight. Here was the first treat, the first weir. It was decided not to go over the rolling bay but at the back of the hatches. Boats were unloaded. All hands ran them across the narrow neck of land and shipped them on the opposite side. The cargo was then replaced. This was all accomplished without any mishap and we were soon afloat again.

The house of his Lordship [Lord Wimborne of Canford Manor] had to be passed and a very dignified position we felt we were in, wading and pushing the boats along, it being far too shallow for us to be aboard. It was just a question of whether we could get by, but at last all was well and we were aboard. It required careful navigation: the water was rocky and broken. As the places were passed, various tales of monster fish being caught were related. Soon the sun bursted out warm and bright and all were in jovial spirits.

This is the Frying Pan

This is the Bacon sketched in Proportion.

The first breakfast, sketched by the Skipper.

We rowed on until a well-known farmhouse at Hampreston appeared, where one of the boats stopped for further provisions in the shape of fresh eggs and milk. The Ad' and myself went on and selected a place for breakfast, it being now nearly 10 a.m. The cooking utensils and requisites were produced, kettle set boiling, rugs spread and, when the others came, the frying pan was produced. Lor! that frying pan: it was so small, one rasher could only be cooked at a time, and that by degrees.

The breakfast was to be bacon and eggs. First course, the bacon, was fished out and, being thoughtful, we had it cut into rashers by the shop people. Such rashers! Thick was a fool to them; long, lean and juicy. One was put into the pan as an experiment. It went on cooking, hissing and spluttering. The fellows began smacking their lips and looking. At the end of five minutes, a thin blue smoke was seen ascending and the hissing sound increased to a crackling. Jimbly was equal to the occasion

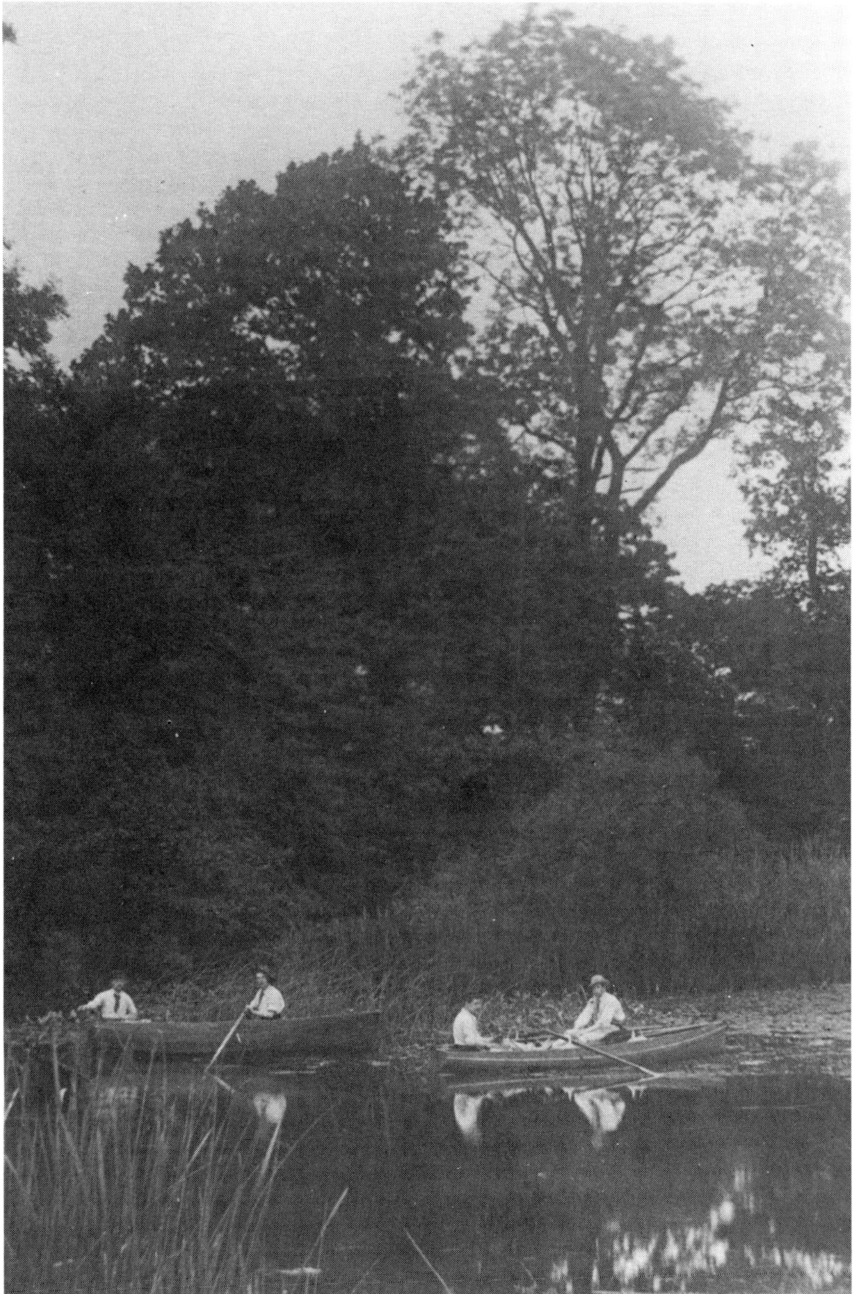

(I always thought he hung round the kitchen door). Knocking things right and left, he scrambled for butter and heaved about a pound into the frying pan, explaining that the pig had no fat in him.

After bacon, then came eggs, coffee, bread and butter, stewed fruit, and a very pleasant meal it proved. After negotiation [of] the river bank to see if any fish were about, we prepared to move on, and here a difficulty appeared. Of course, no-one thought of the washing-up of platters etc. We were too full to do as the little ditty directs – "Lick the platters clean" – and no dish cloths or towels were provided. First we tried the river but the grease would not come off, although we appealed with kind words and unkind words. So we had to boil water to wash them; the wiping had to be done without; the knives and forks were dug into Mother Earth, who cleaned and restored them nicely.

It was a glorious morning, not a cloud was now visible. The banks on either side were one mass of foliage, the trees reaching down to the water's edge a thousand coloured greens, and the smaller vegetation fringed the banks, the tall graceful iris nestling in the spear beds and reeds, the gaudy water lilies, with the innocent forget-me-not. All appealed to the eye and awoke the sense of the beautiful, the birds

At Hampreston "two capital views were obtained". Photos by Arthur Kerridge.

flitting to and fro and singing, the butterfly on the wing, the splash and cry of the waterfowl, the murmur of the bee, all nature in its glory. Yes! It is good for us to be here; the soothing effect, the feeling of intense happiness invaded us all.

My friends! All things in this world are transitory. (I mention this in case you've mislaid your Bible.) We might have known such extreme happiness could not last; nor did it, but there were no Mark Tapley's aboard, and if we had known the near future, the pleasure would have been marred.

We arranged for the front boat to be occupied by three, two rowing, one at the tiller, to be relieved every hour. It was pleasant travelling – one could lay back and listen to the lazy splash of the oars. The ripples, catching the full blaze of the sun, shone like gold. It was hot and as the sun got higher, even oppressive, making the water appear beautifully cool, various feet could be seen hanging over the gunwale and stern. Socks and boots were things unknown – we were away from the ills of civilization, stiff shirts and collars, boots and shoes, and as happy as sandboys.

"What ...? What's that?" Sounds like civilization.

"It's those d......d weeds," heartily exclaims a voice.

Yes, too true. Those weeds! It was the first of a series of exclamations and they have a lot to answer for. They'll surely be burnt. It's a wonder they weren't on the spot – the epitaphs bestowed on them reeked of

The Stour and cottages at Longham, c. 1950.

brimstone. They were weeds, too. Long, lanky weeds, medium weeds, short weeds, fat weeds, in fact every sort of weeds. But they had one thing in common – a propensity for clinging, and they did it well. Shake them off? Oh, no. You couldn't do it. They weren't to be shaken off and well we believed it. They literally sucked at the oars. However, hope buoyed us up. It was child's play to what was to come, on the return journey, but we must not anticipate.

"Skip, I'm going to take this."

Don't be frightened, Reader. He wasn't going to pocket some land. It was the voice of the Big Un, who had taken his camera and was about to take a view. The camera and paraphernalia was put ashore and two capital views were obtained.

As yet, they don't tax one for taking views, but in these advanced days, where man daren't walk on God's earth except the highways, there's no knowing when they will.

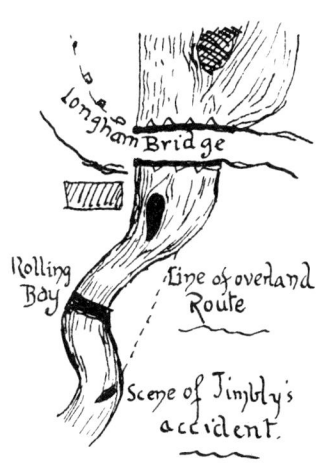

The Skipper's map of Longham.

Soon the rumbling of thunder was heard, the air was very oppressive and sky overcast. This made us set to work in earnest, it being resolved to camp below Longham. After many a weary stroke, the waterworks houses with their summerhouse appearance were in sight. Here was another treat, another weir. However, the cargo was once more discharged and the boats lifted and hauled at a double across the land and launched again. The cargo was then once more replaced, all accomplished with much alacrity, to the astonishment of the occupants of the cottages near the bridge.

There was one stirring incident. The lighter boat, before we crossed over the land, was sent to find a suitable landing place. Jimbly was perched up in the bow sitting on the gunwale facing the stern, looking very grand and sailor-like, he thought. His attention was attracted by the admiring cottagers when the boat touched the bank and rebounded. Jimbly was taken unawares and jerked off the bow gunwale and post into space (I mean the sitting part of him). Luckily his feet caught in the stringers of the ribs and he managed to save himself. The position he was in was most ludicrous, waving his arms frantically and spluttering and muttering for help. A hearty laugh was all the help afforded him, and it proved sufficient.

With the aid of friendly hands from some of the workmen repairing the bridge, we got safely over the shallows and proceeded on our way. The weather was now perfectly beastly — cold, cloudy and inclined for rain. The spirits had to be broached to keep us warm.

It was now after 3 p.m. and the first suitable place we saw we were to camp at. We soon saw a pretty place sheltered by trees and high ground

First and last camp, Dudsbury. Left to right: Jenvey, Skipper Brett, Murray Kerridge, Will Brett. Photo by Arthur Kerridge.

The Stour at Dudsbury, c. 1912. Photo by Sir Kaye le Fleming.

at the back. It was to be the first camping place (and last one, too, curiously enough). In a few minutes, we were busy pitching the baggage, tent, provisions and paraphernalia ashore. Some devoted themselves to collecting sticks. The Big Un, assisted by Jimbly, were engaged in laying out the canvas. (By the by, I can't say too much for the amount of work the Big Un did. Wherever there was hard work, there you would find him. If you contemplate an expedition, take him as a useful accessory. There is one drawback, and I can't quite decide on which side the balance falls, although I've done miles of calculation to arrive at the answer, i.e. is the amount of work he does equal to the amount of work he causes by means of the extra grub, consequently extra cooking, not to mention expense, then again extra weight? Not only himself but everything appertaining to him is on a gigantic scale. It takes a lot of arithmetic to arrive at the result. I had carefully calculated his rowing capabilities and found it exactly came out at one donkey power, which I have every reason to believe is correct. Then I set to work to find the extra amount of weight caused by his presence. There was his carcase and clothing, all of which I calculated. The one thing that upset the calculations was Nestle milk. I was stumped, nor could I arrive at any conclusion. "If half a pot of condensed milk is soaked into a pair of trousers, what is the average amount of weight added, spread over a period of seven days?" That was the question. There are many things to be taken into consideration in working it out, which complicates and leads to more questions. There's evaporation, consequent to its exposure to air; additions, owing to the presence of dirt, dust, microbes, etc; alterations, caused by scraping with a pocket knife to endeavour to remove some of it. All these things and others undermentioned tend to vitiate and make void the original calculation, so I leave in despair the task.)

The Ad' and self were unloading the boats and bringing the necessaries ashore when the news was suddenly brought us that a man was bearing down on us at a terrific rate; and soon the cracking of the bushes, giving forth the sound as if an enraged bull was dashing headlong, confirmed the report.

"Now then! Who gave you permission to be here?"

Everybody, who were most ardently at work (it was agreed in sotto voice to go on until the disturbing element arrived), dropped whatever they were doing and assumed the most innocent appearance [and] looked up. Not a word was spoken. The attack was quite too much.

"Be off with you." Such impudence was never heard of. "Who are you, I should like to know?" and other ejaculations delivered at the highest pitch of anger.

But still not a word. The situation was, to say the least of it, creepy and to an onlooker must have been most ludicrous.

The Big Un, with mallet in hand, gave the only sign of life by his hard breathing and nervous twitching of hand. I was afraid he would smite the disturber. The others might have been transformed suddenly into pillars of salt. Certainly their faces wore that expression. I think the silence was good – it must have acted as an antidote to the enraged one. I meekly mumbled something – to this day I don't know what it was. However, it brought forth a stinging retort, which makes me think as I have stated, that silence was best.

"Where do you come from? Where are you going? Have you come through Canford Water? Nobody stopped you? You are disturbing the ducks. Have you a dog?" and a quantity of further questions were put, at first answered by one, but as the confidence increased the answers were taken up by the entire company in chorus.

We politely informed the gentleman, if he chucked us off, we should camp lower down. He replied with the comforting answer: "Well, you'll get stopped at Lord Malmesbury's water. You can never get through," adding, "Well! There, boys, if I let you stop, you won't run about and do any damage, will you?"

We all replied strongly: "No, sir."

It was all ended, the great ordeal gone through, and we were alive. Perhaps the old gentleman remembered he once was a boy, too. Poor man. We bear him no malice and I think each one of us felt sorry when we heard of his death which has since occurred. "May the dust lie lightly on his grave."

The spirits of the party were now down to zero. We collected in a little group to discuss the situation, though why I don't know. The cheerful shout and whistle was gone; all felt a degree of depression. The remark that we could never get through somewhat dismayed us. The Big Un to the rescue: "Well, you are some chaps! I never! Well, there! Wait till we're turned back, then grumble," setting a good example by driving the pegs in until they split asunder.

The tent was pitched, rugs and sails spread over the grass to keep off the damp, kettle on the fire and things a bit shipshape, then a meal prepared and eaten, followed immediately by a brew of Scotch. Down came the rain, a beastly, nasty drizzle, and cold as polar regions, and to tell the truth the evening was getting too monotonous. If something didn't turn up (Micawber) suicide was inevitable. Something did turn up – a dawg, a cur truthfully, but we were pleased to see him. Soon his master appeared, a bit surprised to see so large a mushroom so early in the year, and a musical one too.

We invited the old man in. After placing the tent and inmates in jeopardy, he got in, and his moon-like face lit up with pleasure as he supped at the flowing bowl, and smacked his lips and rolled his beady eyes.

"Ha'n't-a sin none of your sort for many a long day, but I can't stop – I be a-coom down to cut a nitch o' vern."

But he did stop, and we related our encounter with the previous visitor.

"Tan't his land," exclaimed the old man. "He only got the shooting. I d' rent the land."

We certainly got wrath at this information, and if the gent had interfered after this, I'm afraid he'd have seen another side of us.

We followed the old man to a few yards from the river bank, where the ground rose precipitously, almost like the side of a ravine, and was covered with stunted trees, gorse, fern, etc. Here the old chap set to work to cut "a nitch o' vern", as he explained. We all had a turn at cutting the "vern", and very good fun it was; it helped the evening on.

1st Camp

Candlestick

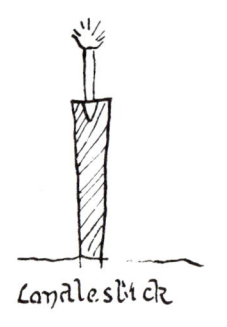

"... *We sat in the dim light of a taller dip.*"

On hearing the old chap kept a pub, there was immediately a suggestion to go with the old man, so the Ad' and Big Un and self journeyed up there and returned with mineral waters. It was so dark and terrible at 8.30, we agreed to close the tent and make snug for the night. As we sat in the dim light of a taller dip, the rain could be heard pattering down on the canvas, and the bigger drop from the trees sounded quite a crash. It jarred on one's nerves and the silence maintained made it more palpable. One thought of a week of similar weather, of a nice cosy club and nice friends, discussing as to how soon we should turn up, if tonight or tomorrow. Never on this earth do I wish to spend another night such as that, nor in another world either, and yet what a beautiful morning!

Somebody introduced cards. There was no inclination to play and they were chucked up. In silence, deep and impressive, was the whisky brewed, and deep and long were the draughts. Yes, it was whisky. Only whisky could appease and satisfy and so whisky it was. It put me in mind of an Irish wake. The wreaths of blue smoke with which the tent was filled twisted themselves into every conceivable shape, and the faces loomed through the smoke, giving the interior a most weird appearance.

The Ad' at last dropped off to sleep after suffering all the evening with a bad head, and we all soon after lay down for the night. As I lay my head on the impromptu pillow (composed of a pair of boots, fishing tackle and a book), an obnoxious smell took hold of me. I analysed that smell. Is it vegetable? No, it's not vegetable; nor animal, but mineral! Yes, it was mineral – petroleum oil! With great skill, I followed up that smell. We had brought no petroleum, I know, as our stove was methylated spirit. How could it come here? I sniffed great sniffs and found it was the sail of one of the boats. The sail having been kept in a house containing a quantity of petroleum, got contaminated. It was the first of the cursed stuff and it followed us all the rest of the time.

The sleeping being pretty general, I joined the majority.

I awoke, however. I don't know if it was that my instinct told me whisky was being toped or that the topers made too much row. Certain it was I woke, and by the dim light I could describe two eerie-looking figures with their capes thrown over their heads, looking very like the monks of old (in more ways than one) as they chuckled to themselves over their roguishness. I claimed my share and was satisfied.

"*A mist hung over the river.*" Photo by Phil Yeomans.

"It was a beautiful morning."
Photo by Phil Yeomans.

Bow woo woo! It's a nasty dream and I turned over when the fishing reel hit into me and informed me it wasn't. Oh! I was so cold and a pale disc could be seen through the canvas like a halo. Curse that dog.

"Well, Jimbly, are ye awake?" It's the voice of the Big Un from an unknown land. "Sleepers awake! Salute the happy morn!"

Half-past-three a.m. and cold as charity, we lay and grumbled, cursing our devilish luck, until the tent was opened. The moon was shining beautiful but a mist hung over the river; the grass to the naked feet was cold as ice. We, however, prepared a brew of Bovril served hot. After, we one by one peeped out and looked about. We set to and prepared breakfast. It was satisfactory to note the sky was clear. Breakfast was cooked, eaten and cleared away by 7 a.m. and the Big Un took a view of the first camp (see plate). It was a very pretty camp but unfortunately it was pitched on ground of somewhat boggy nature and inhabited by creeping animals.

It was a beautiful, bright, cloudless morning as we shoved off and our spirits rose, further increased by a beautiful, clear stretch of water. We

Throop Mill, c. 1900.

lay down on the tent and rugs, spread out, when off duty, in the stern boat, and it was beautiful. The river banks swarmed with notice boards. My only regret is time would not permit us to take views of them, as they would have formed an interesting collection of different specimens of prohibitive notices, and there's no knowing when we may require to put up some on our own estates.

"Hullo! What station's this?"

"It's no station."

"I know 'tis. Anyway, you don't see many railway coaches off the line."

It was a railway coach transferred into a summerhouse, a novel sight, rather.

On we went, past farmhouses and notice boards. However, we eluded the vigilance of the keepers.

Throop Mill was sighted and when we came to it, we asked permission, which was granted, and we proceeded to negotiate the third and last weir. It was a very awkward job, as the banks were high. However, all was safely accomplished, the three bars crossed and we were afloat. Now, boys, to Christchurch straight away (but it proved anything but straight)!

The wildfowl began to rise and create such a noise as to cause some little discomfort as we were approaching Heron Court, where the river is strictly preserved, and the old man's warning was to come to pass. We

Heron Court, home of Lord Malmesbury.

rowed silently past the house and were just congratulating ourselves when a duck punt appeared in sight, lustily propelled along.

"Lord Malmesbury's orders, gentlemen, to stop all boating."

"Can't help that," is the reply, and we pull on.

The man follows and kindly enquired if we had seen any other keepers.

"Oh, dear, no! And don't want to!"

A running fire is kept up, when the man sees the folly of it. So, singing out that a row of piles would successfully accomplish what he had failed to do, he turned and punted upstream.

That man was a coward and a liar and caused us much anxiety looking for piles that didn't exist. That man has caused me seriously to think of spiritualism, too. I want to torment him by my presence in the shape of a pile; a pointed one. I haven't quite succeeded yet but I'm studying Annie Besant, the late Madame Blavatsky and other Theosophical students, including Mr. Stead. If I succeed, that man will have a happy time.

Again the weather changed. It was thundering and a drop or two of rain came. It was the invoice of a lot more.

Somehow or other, during the last overland business, a tin of Nestles' milk which was opened got misplaced and some of it got on to the seat (the floor was big enough for it). Nor did it content itself with one seat but got on to another sort of seat and there it stayed the whole time. Perhaps it's there now? But we hope otherwise, for the sake of the wearer.

Raining hard again. The Ad' and Jimbly in the stern boat put on their mackintoshes and covered up the cargo. The Long Un was pulling bow and myself stroke and the long and the short of it was a wetting. The man at the helm was blue with cold. Not a sound was audible, save a hushed curse on the Clerk of the Weather, and the munching of lunch biscuits which the inmates of the stern boat would exasperatingly do in spite of us.

The windings of that river was awful. We doubled, twisted, came back and went forward. I supposed the river knew its end was nigh (which it wasn't) hence the contortions.

We got wet through in the first boat and then they handed us our coats. There was great dissatisfaction against some unknown authority, and some known authorities, too. The weeds grew troublesome and they were called ugly names; so were the landlords for allowing them to grow.

Iford Bridge, c. 1900.

After an hour's rowing, a windmill came in sight (bad cess to it), then disappeared and came again until we thought it was possessed or a will-o'-the-wisp. At last, however, we came up to it. There it was, blowing and turning, revelling and delighting itself at our expense and laughing and chattering right merrily in the rain.

However, on, on, on. Iford Bridge at last! I was simply doubled up with rowing but still it was on, on, on! The Long Un was very gentle; his consideration for me was very beautiful; it was such a contrast to the harsh words the other ones in the stern boat used against us for not rowing faster. What they said was cruel but he bore it for me without a murmur. I don't think about it too often as it overcomes me.

The wind was blowing a gale and it was with great difficulty we made headway. As we passed the railway bridge, two fellows in a skiff caught sight of us, buffeting against wind and water. They lay on their oars until we were abreast of them, then they fled. It was the fascinating looks of the crew. They asked themselves, "What manner of man is this?" and it was unanswerable.

Another bridge and then, thank God, the ferry, where we waited some time in the rain for the people to instruct us what to do, much to their amusement. We hadn't had quite enough rain, I suppose. We talked to the ferryman and ferrymaid and they were kind and took the boats in charge. We then selected what personal belongings we should require – change of raiment, provisions and that very necessary article drink.

Armed thus, five weary, wretched, dripping, unshorn, sweet-tempered fellows, all sorts and sizes, tramped the streets of Christchurch (of course, we went the wrong end of the town) in search of a restaurant. The inhabitants came to their doors and asked questions one to another as to the locality of the shipwreck. A mob of small boys escorted part the way asking if a menagerie had broke loose, which was rude. We found a show, however, and after a wash and change, did full justice to a meal, and make arrangements for the night.

It was not too long before the Big Un had found his way to the nearest pub and we all followed. Nothing but drink, now. We went in a body and were shown to the smoking room. Jimbly stayed behind with the barmaid until an old gent appeared, who called in a deep, husky voice for "a glass of the best and dryest and a sugar Mary" and accompanied him to the smoking room.

We opened our hearts to that old man and he opened his memory to us (such a long one!) until a fellow came in and talked politics. We don't talk politics as a rule.

The studied attitudes of the crew, the painfully attentive way they listened, was only too apparent. The forcible "Now, Sir, I maintain" of the old man and the way he eyed one when so speaking was too much for some of the crew. It seemed incumbent for them to make some reply and they did so faintly, upon which the old man eyed them still more and asked them to repeat it. Then their presumption became apparent, their powers of elocution failed, embarrassment speedily terminated what indiscretion had begun. He was too much for us, but a kind old man: gave us free use of the hotel grounds and lawn tennis courts. We used the grounds but not the courts, and they were pretty grounds, and good.

In the early evening letters were indulged in, one to the great and mighty, the owner of riparian rights, to wit one Malmesbury of an earldom in his own right, and before the travellers could begin the journey home it must so please the mighty one that they might do so. With many humbles, obedients and servants, the epistle was dispatched on its errand; and lo, when two days had passed, writing was found at the appointed place conveying that it so pleased this bulwark of the constitution to allow, grant and permit his humble lieges to return.

We afterwards found a Constitutional Club and the people, not all being such heathens as they looked, had compassion on us and took us in, and the remainder of the evening was passed in playing billiards, and it was good.

It was also good turning into blankets and we slept uncommonly well and long. After breakfast we took various views with the camera. The rain held off but it was blowing heavily. A blue sky could be seen in places so we decided, after a good meal, to push on to Mudeford. We purchased a few necessaries, paid off all scores and made for the boats, stowed the provisions on board, got all direction from the ferryman and started once more.

The river now became very broad. We proceeded in independent order, as it was blowing so rough. The waves were white-crested and the spray came flying aboard. Not knowing a bit the proper course, but trusting in God as all good mariners do, we made way.

It is no easy matter to navigate mud flats, especially when friendly advice is given you to go straight on the mud. The consequence was we got grounded several times. Twix many a shave, we got to the haven mouth, where a brass band, flags and crowds of people were congregated.

"The Haven consisted of two or three tumbledown Irish-looking houses..."

The Skipper's sketch of a toy tree.

"We didn't a bit expect this nor want it," said one member, who thought it was all in his honour.

Our boats coming along perfectly regardless of a retreating tide and shoals of mud, the matter-of-fact way when the boats got stuck how the crew simply got out and shoved them off as though it was the most ordinary daily occurrence, caused no little wonder amongst a knot of old salts, and when we got abreast, the regatta, for such it proved to be, quite stopped, the interest being transferred to us.

No-one had the least idea of what Mudeford or the Haven was. Their ignorance was soon dispelled. The Haven consisted of two or three tumbledown Irish-looking houses on a narrow, sandy, flat peninsular with a bit of strap grass in the centre, sporting a few stunted pine trees and scraggy furze, surrounded by that diabolical invention barb wire, which put one in mind of the toy gardens you buy composed of board sanded and thin red sticks with round bottoms and dyed mop top for trees, stamped "Made in Germany". Altogether, it looked a most inviting place.

There was a-talk of pitching camp inside the barb' wire. Some didn't like the idea and we got ashore on the sea wall to discuss and look about, much to the disgust of a pair [young couple]. The lady immediately put her parasol to hide vision of something. Since, I think it was the Admiral's legs, which were bare!

We decided to go on and we put off again and rowed until we were out to sea; at least, I mean beyond the river's mouth. The coast was bound by a cliff and a nice sandy beach 200 yards from high water mark. We found a nice place by the side of a boathouse, where the cliff was only twenty feet high. Indeed, it was more like a bank and covered with grass and sheltered to a great extent. The sand a good way to the sea was covered with strap grass.

"... on a narrow, sandy flat peninsular..."

The boats were hauled up on shore and the cargo and necessaries brought to the foot of the cliff. It was laborious work under a hot sun. By the time tent was pitched and things put shipshape, it was 5 o'clock. Luckily there was a house near to supply us with water. Jimbly and the Welshman strolled off there for some water. They came back skipping like lambs, with a can of water – hot, too, as they explained – and tales of wondrous girls at the house (and it was truly wonderful what that house supplied us with).

An old bucket with the bottom missing was extemporized for a fire receptacle and a few old lobster pots caught napping made famous fuel. We cooked and had a pleasant meal and with our pipes we were happy once again.

It being Wednesday, two more of the pious brothers and a friend had arranged that day to come and visit us, so the Admiral and self started off to the nearest pub (in this case, the Haven House). To look elsewhere, we had learnt by experience, would be a waste of time.

They were not to be seen, however, nor could we learn any account of them, although we looked all over the place and in nooks and crannies. They were there or thereabouts, so they say. From that, we can draw our own inference.

We amused ourselves by watching the boatloads of babies, evidently born amphibious creatures; creatures of two years misery treating eighteen-months-old passengers on trips, the passengers tumbling and crawling one over the other like blind kittens. It was all very well until the bow man caught a crab. Then the yell that went up from those little dears could not be equalled in any inferno. The elders, most of them, were under the genial influence of that most patronized god Bacchus [the Greek god of wine] and brawlings were not scarce, so to avoid nasty things we made for camp.

On our arrival we found the three gazing out to sea, and soon we were gazing also. It was beautiful watching the sun, perfectly crimson, sinking behind the chain of hills to the west, and the unfamiliar music of the gentle roll of the waves and the faraway sound as they stretched away in the distance. The cliffs of the Isle of Wight opposite blazed with the last touches of the sun; the steely expanse of water and the unequalled colour of the sky formed a picture never to be forgotten. It filled us with something we couldn't understand. We gazed on until the splendid panorama faded and the cliffs became a dark blue and the lights of the lighthouses embedded in them appeared and disappeared, warned us if there was anything to do before turning in, it must be done. With a feeling of unexplainable vacancy tinged with regret, we wandered

"... *sporting a few stunted pine trees and scraggy furze ...*"

slowly to our tent. Alas! how soon these feelings of a better sort soon leave us.

No sooner than we were within the tent and rugs spread, cards were produced and the flowing bowl went merrily around and nap proceeded with shouts of joy.

During the evening, people could be heard like hyaenas prowling around. We took no notice until somebody got mixed with the ropes, causing the tent to pitch and roll. Then it was out and at 'em!

The authors of all this trouble were three youths. Not knowing what to do with them, they were asked inside. They just took to whisky like ducks to water and that extravagant Jimbly brewed bowl after bowl, much to our discomfort, and to the others' discomfort afterwards, but it made them conversant and they informed us as to their weekly income, occupations and general capacity.

After a long discussion on political economy, we could see from the manner [in which] one of them tried to put out the candle with the assistance of his pipe that the time had arrived for a song. After much deliberation, one of them sang a song. It was a very touching song in its way, about a soldier and a young lady, introducing a third party as time went on. We loudly applauded the performer and wetted his other eye. His success induced the second one, after much persuasion, to warble forth. It was something of a sailor. The state of the gentleman caused some disturbance in his articulation, consequently much of the beauty of the song was lost; but it didn't matter — we were impartial in our applause.

"No, Bill, it be thy turn!"

"I tell thee I can't zing."

"Thee't zing! Thees's know — was't zung t'other night!"

Bill was the gent who was trying to put the candle out. It appeared to his vision to be variating in size, causing him to blink like an owl, and called attention to its peculiar manner. However, after another pull to clear his throat, he began. As the song went on, Bill's memory got worse and his eyeballs began to jingle, howsome'er we helped him, each member of the company singing his own tune, and Bill a different one to himself. The chorus, as far as we could catch, was:

> *"The oak and the ash and the bonny willow tree,*
> *They all grow together in the North Country."*

The rest sank into oblivion. The last straw had broken the camel's back. Bill sank a helpless mass to the ground. We roused him and got him and his companions on the outside and underway. Whilst leading him,

Jimbly tried to explain to the young man he was all right, which he agreed to. During the slight pauses, he desisted from depositing our whisky on the sand. It was a simple waste of pure liquor; when I'm stony broke I recall it to mind.

After seeing the visitors on the way home, in the interests of mankind (they were specimens pure and simple you don't meet every day and we led them some distance lest they fell into the sea), we turned in and laced up for the night, adjusted rugs, put on top coats and sleeping apparel and lay down. Time 11.15 p.m.

I had brought a book to while away the time and, by the aid of the taller [candle], commenced to read. It was a bad job. Boots, candle, book, myself, odds and ends of various sorts got mixed and the flying articles dangerous, so in regard to the others I gave up.

"Ugh! Ugh!"

"Good morning, gentlemen."

When I opened my eyes and senses came, there was a conversation going on and the tent open. Some were holding conversation with one of the coastguardmen. Time: 4 a.m. Grass beastly wet with dew and air mortal chilly, the island was surrounded in haze. As we gazed across the broad Channel, whilst boiling water for some Bovril, we played duck, which warmed us considerably.

"... Altogether, it looked a most inviting place."

The Ad' and self took a plunge into the briney, to the amusement and jeers of the others. Will came in after. It was a very warm job.

We cooked a breakfast of bacon in detachments. The frying was very delicate work with the small pan and required the nicest handling to keep the sand out of the dishes. After the meal, at about 7 a.m., a photograph of the camp was taken by me (at least, I took the cap off and put it on again), Jimbly previously effectively writing in a conspicuous place the well-known "FAR FROM THE MADDING CROWD". It would have been far more applicable, as things turned up, if he had written "Near to the Madding Crowd".

Jimbly, after the meal, might have been seen dickying up. He was going to leave us. He had business at Swanage, as he explained. I should like to follow the same sort of business – I think it must be very profitable. Emergency is the principal thing, I should think, as it couldn't be put off on any account, he explained. I don't like to be personal but it's the very first business I've known that Jimbly couldn't put off.

The Ad' and myself took upon us to row him in or, to be more correct, we allowed him to row himself in. There was a gentle breeze, not too hot, and Jimbly, being in good fettle at the prospect of business, rowed along right merrily. We moored to the quay and went into the town and wished Jimbly every success in the business and he left us.

We then procured letters, papers, including a copy of Funny Folks for the Big Un, and some provisions, and then set off to find a Mr. Tucker, whom we were recommended to call on for information as to fishing. A very nice gentleman he was, and went to a lot of trouble on our account, advised us as to the best place, gave us a sketch of the spot, state and time of tide, lent us some rope and a killie, also some fishing lines. When you consider we were total strangers, it was more than ordinary. We bought some more fishing tackle for making up. Armed with this, we rowed back.

During our absence, the Big Un and Will had renewed their acquaintance with the coastguards and had obtained their permission to use the boathouse for to grub in. This was a welcome acquisition, as the sand had become intolerable, to say nothing of various crawling animals which we called sand diggers. Flesh diggers would have been more appropriate.

We found them on their backs in the tent – which was as hot as a furnace, despite the walls being rolled up – too lazy to move or talk or do anything, so we just lay down and did the same.

There was a chatting audible, so we turned out to see what it was. There were two gentlemen, one say past forty and the other about thirty

The permanent camp at Avon Beach, Mudeford, showing (left to right) Jenvey, Murray Kerridge, Arthur Kerridge, Will Brett. Photo by Skipper Brett.

or a little over. The first gentleman was very busy extracting balls of many coloured worsted from one pocket, unrolling them, then rolling them up again and transferring them to the other pocket. This peculiar gentleman was accompanied by another whose chief occupation appeared to be gnawing his finger. We shortly afterwards learnt that these poor fellows were idiots. They afforded us immense amusement, however. Perhaps it was wrong of us to extract it from them but we certainly meant no harm.

When the coastguard appeared, he set them to work to dig for gold, as he explained. They rummaged the sand with their sticks and poked about and after a lot of fuss produced some coppers (previously placed there by the coastguard). This appeared to be their one delight. They asked us to dig, too, which we undoubtedly had done if we thought we should find gold. But our lack of faith prevented us.

Whilst watching the white sails of the yachts cruising in the bay, one could moralize on these sad incidents. Are we much better than they? Are we more sane? Some will think not. All our existence is spent in raking in, or trying to, and these poor chaps had only the same desire. And yet if you don't rake in, what then? What alternative? In these competetive days, the fight is for life. You have to. There is no alternative. It is sad, especially for us who have no wish for rank or smell, who only desire to be well fed, clothed, housed and have every luxury, and let alone. We don't wish much and yet it is denied us. We must legislate for measures! The course of the world must be changed! I say, young men, join us, unite, congregate in one immense implacable body; level classes of every kind; shake the foundations of this unholy, cursed existence. Kill, I say, and spare not the hand of the despoilers; throw off the yoke; let men be men in one vast and universal brotherhood, sharing each other's burdens, and journey hand in hand in this our first stage of existence. Let equality, fraternity and socialism be our password as we march on to our Utopian dreams, sure to be accomplished by the great socialistic and radical movement of today provided one thing happens, and which until then men may prate for ever and ever, or until the millenium comes, when humanity will be just without fear of the law, good without fear of the judgement day, moral without fear of the curse of sin. Without this, the dream is the result of selfish morbidness and an unjust desire to possess some of the worldly wealth which exists in the hands of others. My friends, spurn all such ideas, labour silently on, crucify the flesh and your reward shall not be empty.

Many and such were the thoughts which came, and then somebody said something about mussels and, after a little food, we went hunting for mussels for bait for the morrow. It was a terrible job, crawling under huge boulders of concrete made accessible by reason of the tide being out. The mussels held on like grim death. It cut one's fingers cruel and a grimy, oozy black smell prevaded one for some hours after.

In the afternoon we wandered along the coast. The Big Un amused himself with watching the ladies bathe. He has an eye for the beautiful; he also has an eye for grub and a stomach to contain it, which earned for him a nasty but truthful sobriquet. He was especially enamoured by a little girl of thirteen years, showing one the truth in the saying

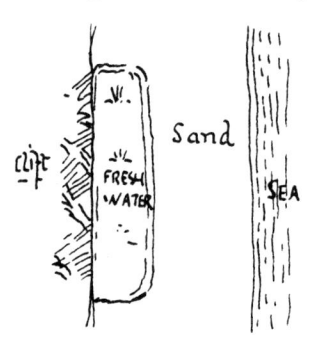

"There was one curious thing we saw – a freshwater lake within a dozen or so yards of the sea."

"extremes meet". It didn't quite satisfy him, as when a larger species turned up, he was just as keen.

We regularly fooled away the afternoon, paddling in the sea, running and mucking about. There was one curious thing we saw – a freshwater lake within a dozen or so yards of the sea. It appears to have been formed by the changing of the river course, which at one time ran along the cliff some considerable distance farther than now, and was protected by sandbanks. During the lapse of time, these have become extinct by the action of the sea and left part of the course extant, which forms the lake. But it is peculiar that the water is not brackish, being so close to the sea. Probably the springs in the cliff feed it. We were told that large quantities of freshwater eels are caught there still.

The coastguards kindly supplied us with crockery and potatoes without our even asking them. Indeed, we had fallen in clover in every way. After the evening meal, further improved by coffee and cream, the gift of the girls from the house, whose many kindnesses in every way cannot be underrated (for particulars ask the Big Un), our acquaintances of the previous evening turned up clothed and in their right minds. Being philanthropists in our way, and having an eye to economy, the whisky was kept snug, and a light drink of claret and lemonade brewed for them. We thought they would probably like to have a meal tonight as a change, so all the remnants and odds and ends of tinned meat etc., served with biscuits, was given them. When once started they went steadily on, filling their mouths till they couldn't see out. No doubt if we had given them enough they would have eaten until they exploded. They made me think of the lions in menageries.

After they had eaten all, they twisted their tongues round, licked their chops, to use a vulgar expression, and generally behaved like animals. After listening to their further biographies, we thought it incumbent on us to preach to them on the fruits of drink and crime, and pointed out to them the perfect happiness which accrues from a life of sobriety and good morals, which they readily listened to (with the aid of the bowl), and let us hope, my friends, that the seed fell into good grounds and will grow up and prosper.

We watched from the shore the lights of the lighthouses and amused ourselves. It was surprising the quiet calm that reigned since that noisy, roistering, blustering Jimbly had cleared out. However, he was to return on the morrow. Another vicissitude of life!

We soon turned in and slept most comfortably, to be awoken about 4.30 by our friends the Coastguard. Will cooked breakfast – in fact, he did most of the cooking, good thanks to him. All the party except myself were off fishing and soon they put off and pulled off for round the head. The next pleasant business for me was to wash up. I tried the sea but the grease defied me. Next I boiled some water, then the spirit for the stove gave out. Jimbly had told me sand would get the grease off. It got it out of sight, anyway. The vessel was covered with a thick coating of sand stuck on to the grease. I had to make a fire and cook hot water, with the aid of which I got off some of the sand and grease and wiped it in Jimbly's bathing towel. The things looked terribly streaky and when the towel got so full of grease and sand as to stick to the utensils, I chucked the job. I wasn't cut out, evidently, for a Mary Ann.

As I'm a-going up to meet Jimbly into the town, now just for a quiet little shave, says I to myself. So, arranging the little glass on one of the studs of the boathouse, I set to work and was doing fairly well when I fancied a shadow crossed the glass, and looking up I beheld one of the peculiar gentlemen of yesterday a-rolling his eyeballs. Vision of a different shave crossed my mind and I went out, at which the gent sheered off. But he had done his worst. The nervous system was completely shattered. I couldn't start fair but dug and cut myself until a tattooed Maori was a fool to me. However, just a drap of the good old crathur with one of the coastguards enabled me to complete after a fashion and, fastening up the boathouse, I launched the small boat and pulled off to Christchurch.

Making fast to the quay, I wandered up the main street when, lor, right aloft was Jimbly and another, the lost Wilkie, as I'm a sinner.

"Am so glad," says Wilkie as he shakes flipper.

But lor! What toffs! Such white trousers and delicate blue stripes! Inwardly, I vowed vengeance. I think Jimbly went home to get a clean shirt really and to get his trousers washed. They were filthy dirty when he left.

I helped them with some of the large parcels which they had brought containing fresh provisions, which were very welcome. We made for the quay and put off. The raptures of delight poor Wilkie was in at the sight of the grand broad river quite alarmed me. He gradually subsided until he got out of the haven mouth, where the swell of the ocean was felt, then, with a spasmodic effort, he burst forth: "Ain't it beau-tiful," and wept. The wonder is he didn't die right out, it being such a celestial contrast to the city of darkness where he had been spending his time the last few days.

However, we arrived safely at the camp and after a little rest put off and anchored a little way from shore and had a good long bathe. Jimbly as usual took a huge dive to deceive the spectators on the cliff and

Expedition visit to Christchurch Castle.

deceived himself by digging his head in the sand. We returned and, with the aid of the Coastguard's glass, made the fishing party out coming round the head. The tide was going out and the breakers dashed over the shoals. We could plainly see the little boat plunge into the green waves and the white spray break aboard. They seemed to be confused as to the best way of making land. The wind was blowing considerable.

They tacked and stood in when slap bang on a shoal. We could see her bumping heavily and regular seas going aboard. The inmates appeared mixed but at length the Big Un took sails down and unstepped mast. They [put] out oars. At last they got in as far as tide would allow. We waded out to meet them. A pretty time we could see they had experienced, wet as drowned rats and just the least bit scared. We looked for the fish, and we had to look, too. Total – six small pout whiting, very different from what we expected.

The Ad' and self rowed into Christchurch in the evening for some spirits and various things. We called on Mr. Tucker and [he] brought down his son, a nice young fellow, and we quickly became friends.

During our absence the six small fish, rendered considerably smaller by cleaning, had been duly cooked, fried in sand and gravy from dishcloth (extemporised towel) – I mean, butter and breadcrumbs –

and when we arrived, there was the remains of one small fish (he had become scattered in frying and you couldn't tell his head from tail), heaped up in fragments in a dish (from the house), perfectly cold and as solid as stone, and a dish of cold soapy potatoes which eat like stale putty. We did the best for ourselves and guest and it was further improved by a gift from the girls at the house of iced coffee, fruit and cream, kindly brought down by one, as we thought, but there were others in the background. Wilkie was immediately gone, and some of the others turned out, including myself.

Now, from my visits to the kitchen door, I had caught sight of a lovely damsel. She was such a nice young thing, with such a sweet, charming, elegant disposition and winsome manner, you can't think! Quite too-too! She was not a small dolly girl but a tall, lithe and graceful young lady. On tiptoe, I could just reach her arm (I tried that much). If her face was just a trifle full and her mouth a wee bit large, what did that matter? I couldn't see it. The only elevation open to my view (owing to her height or my shortness) was a full double chin, a celestial nose and the crown of a wee blue hat which at an angle of sixty degrees appeared charming.

I thought she cared for me, as she said sweet things to me and spoke softly to me, quite like a child. All these things I attributed to her innocence and sweet nature. I thought of how I would tell her of the Babes in the Wood, Alice in Wonderland, Cinderella and pretty tales like that, and I had tried to remember Goody Twoshoes. Oh, Nellie! I shall never be happy again, but I generously forgive you. I don't think it was all your fault. 'Twas more my misfortune and the fault of someone else. He made a nasty remark and told me 'twas bedtime and then he took her away from me. I daren't say anything 'cause he only laughed at me and said I shouldn't dangle, and grievous words I've been taught stir up anger. So I went back to the tent. I felt white but I didn't cry. After I had eaten nearly the whole of the fruit and cream, I felt better.

After some time, that nasty Big Un returned. Then he teased me. I've lost much of my respect for him since then and if he continues to tease me, as he is still doing, I shall lose all, and I don't want to do that.

We then adjourned from the boathouse to the tent, where we indulged in nap and drank some brews of Scotch etc., which friend Tucker was kind enough to bring. A merry evening was spent, the party now numbering seven, including Wilkie.

We went part the way with Tucker, who promised to spend the morrow evening with us. Before turning in, members might be seen lugging what looked in the dim light like Dutch cheeses from the

The Skipper's fishing sketch.

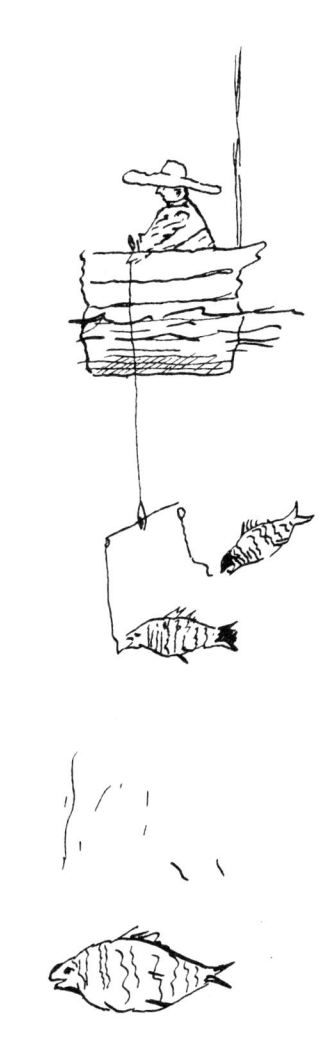

boathouse to the tent. It was only coils of ropes for pillows, and beautiful they were to sleep on – anything rather than lay your head flat on the ground at the same level as your body. I can tell you this from experience. After a round or two more of the flowing bowl, we turned in and slept beautifully.

We awoke moderately early in the morning. It was another beautifully fine morning, with a fine haze over the sea. We had arranged another fishing expedition, the Admiral volunteering to stay home and keep an eye on the tent.

So all us others, after a square meal, put off about 9 a.m. for the fishing ground round Warren Head (see map) into Bournemouth Bay, first, however, going up the haven and procured a supply of mussels for bait from one of the longshoremen. We saw Tucker senior aboard a small sailing boat ahead of us and we couldn't do better than follow their course.

There were not sufficient lines for all of us so one of us opened the mussels and baited in turns. The first place we anchored at was evidently not quite the feeding ground, as we could see the other boat pulling them in by the dozen, so we shifted our moorings, Tucker senior kindly shouting directions from the other boat.

By jove! It was grand hauling them in one after the other, the double hooks two at a time. If there's one thing above all others calculated to make a man a Christian, and satisfied with his lot in this world (that is, provided he has any soul whatever), it's fishing when the sport is good. Why! the remembrance of that morning has buoyed me up through many a weary toil and still will, I hope. We all were elated, even to Jimbly.

"Now this is what I d' call sport," says he. "None of your danged waiting and putting your bait in front of 'em. And you can talk as much as you like. Different to them blooming roach."

Jimbly caught a roach once. Such a roach! We were fishing near the suspension bridge, Canford, one day with ill luck. Jimbly all at once came running back for a piece of bait (worm to wit). Procuring same, off he set at a run. We watched him gently manipulate his rod and then a jerk enough to strike a whale.

"I've got him!" and Jimbly brings him forward. He was a large fish, very large, but no doubt whatever ill, dangerously ill. This could be seen from his flabby look. I think it must have been jaundice or gangrene he was suffering from, poor fish! It may seem cruel but there is no doubt it all happened for the best.

"He didn't bite free, don't yer know," says Jimbly. "I let the hook float down to him. It caught his tail once and the next time went clean into his mouth. Then I pulled. He never moved — came up quietly. From observations, I don't think he quite intended to take the bait. It floated into his mouth unawares. In fact, the only intimation given him when he was hooked was by the sudden jerk. The only response he gave was to turn up the whites of his eyes. From this, and the fact that he was away from all other fish, lying quite still in shallow water by weeds, makes me think he was unwell. He was never cooked. The last I saw of him was on the mixen [dung heap] with a cat looking and smelling him, gently putting out a paw and turning him over. From the reverent way the cat handled him, I feel my theory's corroborated."

The suspension bridge, Canford Magna.

It was a good job the bait gave out at last, as there is no doubt whatever we should have gone on catching them until they sank us. The floor of the boat was heaped high with fish and we ourselves were sitting on fish, mussels and one another, covered with scales and bait. An oozy, slimy smell pervaded us for some time after.

The view was delicious and the gentle movement of the waves soothing and beneficial. We could see Boscombe and Bournemouth piers and the coast right away up the Solent.

Thud! Thud! Thud! The air seemed to vibrate. Out at sea it was hazy and for some time we could make out nothing. Presently there loomed out the lines of some steamer, which turned out to be *The Monarch*. It was novel for us to be really on the sea in the old, despised *Cock-a-Hoop;* and to actually pass a steamer, a known one, to ... lor! Why sometimes I think it must have been a dream – a mighty pleasant one.

The tide began to turn shortly after noon. We up sails and made for Mudeford. Oh! it was delicious. It was Paradise regained. I want nothing better. It was soul satisfying.

A good long reach was made before standing in. When we touched, the Ad' came down and met us. His face wore a look of blank disappointment. Our luck astounded him. When counted, they totalled up sixty-and-two pout whiting. They were rather a white elephant – we didn't know how to get rid of them. After sorting out a couple of dozen of the best, we disposed of the rest to our friends – the two madmen, coastguards and ragged urchins of the place. A light meal ended the morning's sport and I can truthfully say a more enjoyable one I never spent. I don't think I ever shall.

During our absence, the Admiral, it appears, went up to the house and, guided by a bevy of damsels, surveyed the whole premises, and us too, by the aid of a fine telescope. What uses that telescope was used for has caused me some uneasiness. He was also provided with sherry and biscuits. I'm glad it wasn't me.

The Chief Officer of the Coastguard came down in a nasty sweat and wanted various information – where the Henery we had come from, what we were doing, who had given us permission to use the boathouse, he should like to know? We supplied him with all details; if it was his pleasure, we could shift.
"Oh, it's all right. You can stop now. Be careful – don't disturb any of the ropes etc. Don't belong to us but Board of Trade. Good morning."
He was gone. These gents don't mean any harm, only like to have due deference paid to their authority.

Soon after 3 p.m. the Big Un and myself took the camera and made Christchurch. We took some very good views, both exterior and

The Constable's House, Christchurch,
photographed by Skipper Brett and Arthur Kerridge.

"It was proposed to take a group of all the members of the expedition ..."
Left to right: Arthur Kerridge, Nellie, Will Brett, Tucker, the cook, Murray Kerridge, Kellaway, Jenvey. Photo by Skipper Brett.

interior. We also took a rise[?] out of that ancient church. It seems in that institution they do not allow photographs of the interior to be taken unless the vicar or senior clergyman has given permission. We applied at the Vicarage for the necessary but the reverend gent was out. The Big Un was not to be defeated by such a minor thing as permission, so we stalked into the Priory, rigged up the camera. A seeding-looking clerk walked up and asked if we had obtained permission. We informed him it had been applied for but the vicar was out, adding: "They referred us to you," which they didn't do. However, vesting the authority in the clerk's person made that gent more pleased at his extension of power, so we stayed. It would have been awkward if the vicar had turned up during the operation of taking, lasting three-quarters-of-an-hour. We are glad he didn't, not from any selfishness but for the poor clerk's sake, who might have got a wigging. However, all's well that ends well. The Big Un was well pleased and paid the fee.

"We don't charge," as the clerk mildly put it, "but persons are expected to give to the restoration fund."

We afterwards called for Tucker junior, who came provided for the night, and then we made for Mudeford.

57

The Tower, Christchurch Priory.
From the North West.

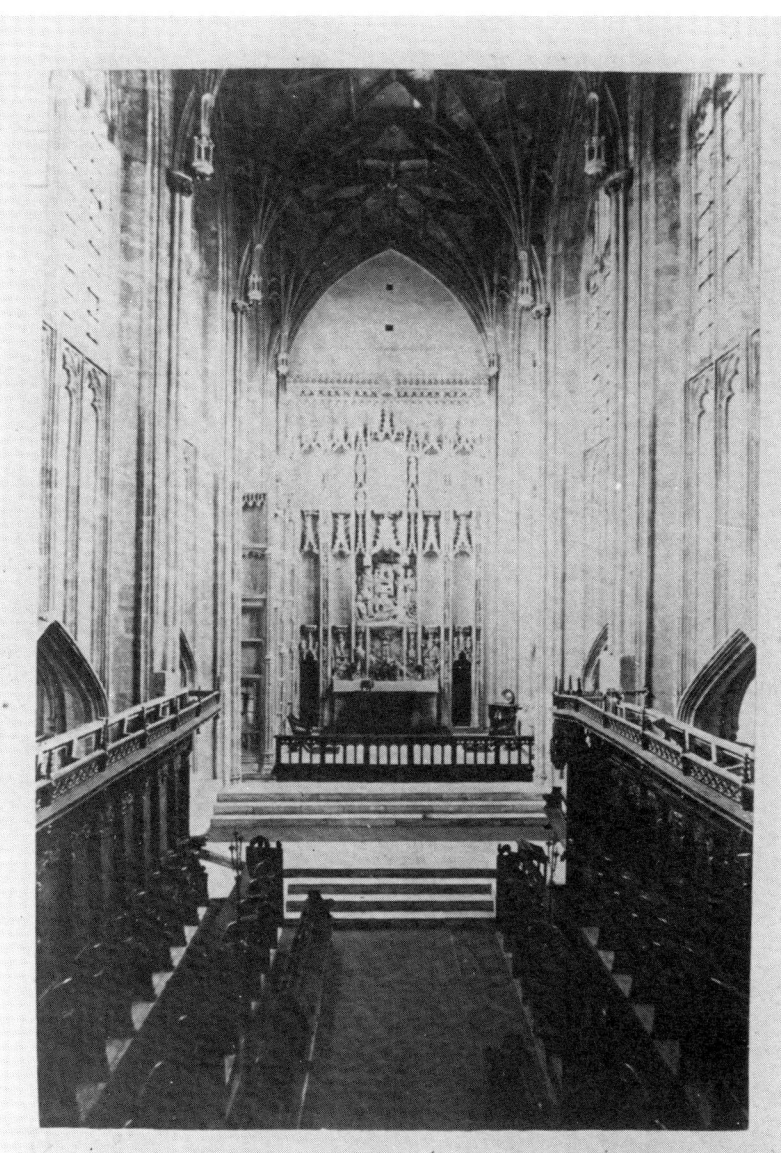

The "Chancel" Christchurch Priory

When we arrived, the Big Un was requested by Nellie to take the photograph of a group composed of the coachman's family and servants. This he readily assented to and arranged the group. I couldn't help admiring the graceful, motherly way Nellie took a little child on her knee, and arranged them all in such nice postures. Showed such taste!

After this, it was proposed to take a group of all the members of the expedition, including Nellie, the cook and Tucker. I thought: "Here's my chance," so I sided up to Nellie in as unpretentious manner as possible. I thought I should like to be taken near her. It wasn't to be. The Big Un came up to me with a scowl.

"Here, Skipper, you can take this one. It'll be the best of all."

I knew it! Too great a presumption on my part ever to think of such a joy. I could see from the malicious smile of the Big Un as he arranged the camera he'd sit on me. So he did. Tried flattery and grubbling. It was useless. He'd made up his mind and I had to take the group. To hide my mortification, I looked through the lens with my eyes shut, holding on to the camera for support.

"Now then, how'll this do?" says he.

I looked through. There he was, sitting with his legs crossed close to Nellie.

"Yes, it'll do," I answered, and adjusted everything prior to taking off the cap. "Are you ready?"

Oh, horror! Just then I saw his arm steal gently round her waist. A thrill [sic] ran through me. "Can I take them?" I said to myself. "Yes. For her sake. For her dead sake." With a white face and trembling hand, I lifted off the cap. It was done. How thankful I was. But oh! how I hated him, and wandered disconsolately off, anywhere, away from them. Suicide came to be clothed as an angel, but I'm so young. "Not just yet," I pleaded.

When I returned, there was a visible commotion going on.

"I say it's pastry – suppose I know," says one.

"No, it's not pastry. It's jelly."

"Jelly be hanged! It's pastry, I tell you. Served up with hashed shrimps and parsley. Isn't it, Skip?"

"How the deuce do I know? What are you quarrelling about?"

After much deliberation, I found the excitement was caused by the cook promising to give us a blow out, it being our last day, and part of the menu was to be an omelet. No-one knew exactly what it was. I don't think we quite know what it is now. But we've tasted, and know of the good and evil; and knowing, we long for more.

The Ad' and myself were deputed to fetch the meal from the house.

We went up and waited round the kitchen door a long time. Then Nellie came and gave us some fruit, which was kind. Yet how cruel to me! Her gentle, soft, languishing manner, quiet, innocent actions, teeming with kindness, caused me many a pang. She was too good for this world; certainly too good for the Big Un. I was sorry for her as well as myself. When I thought of it, a big lump came in my throat, so I went round a corner and pretended to play with a cat I saw there. But I looked so bleary at the cat he ran away.

"It's ready, Skip," shouts the other, so I followed him into the kitchen.

They loaded him with a large dish of bacon and eggs, covered round with a snow-white tablecloth, and they put spoons into his pocket, real silver ones, too. Then they gave me a vegetable dish containing potatoes and green peas, also nicely covered up in linen, and put forks into my pocket. I thought those spoons and forks meant something. In fact, it reminded me of Joseph and his brother, who went down into Egypt to buy corn and found their money returned in their sacks. They let us out by a side door and we had to go by the front of the house round the sea wall. I didn't like a bit the job – it looked so bad with the family plate sticking out of one's pockets. We bobbed down low going by the house and the smell coming through encouraged us to keep on and faith would soon lead to sight.

How those fellows prowled and danced round us, wanting to see what we had long before we got to the boathouse where the blow out was to be.

"Where's the omelet?"

"What's it made of?"

"Haven't got it, so don't upset the bally lot."

"Was it a bogey? Ain't we really going to have one?"

"Yes, if you'll wait, and the girls will bring it down."

"Huroo! So much the better." That was the Big Un.

The dishes were arranged as neat as possible and the table looked quite nice with the silver, linen, crockery and glass. A row or two of empty bottles were arranged in sight by Jimbly. His idea is show and effect but we had one or two for use.

Wasn't the bacon just done to a turn? Real Hampshire hog! And the crown of rich gold of the eggs and silver frilling looked tempting. It was an artistic dish. And the colour of those peas! Oh! such a beautiful green!

"And so young and fresh," says Wilkie.

Jimbly mumbled, between huge mouthfuls, something ... first square meal he'd had.

It was soon all gone, even the gravy. Then they fell to discussing the omelet, looking out every minute to see if it was on the road. At last it came, brought down by the cook in person, who confided to the Big Un Nellie wanted him at the house. Off he went, never even looked at the omelet. I wonder he went off like that, although I'd have given up fifty omelets for Nellie. I didn't think he would. Afterwards I asked him what made him give it up.

"Oh, I had something better," says he.

I expect it was more fruit and cream, 'cause I know she was kind to him.

I can't describe the omelet. It's beyond me. Suffice it to say it appeared a bleary, jellicose mass of yellow orchre, dotted here and there with currants. It made me think of a frying pan with a flabby, jelly, fishy, eggy, oysterish, slimy body following shiveringly the course of a fork round and round until it seemed suspended on the point.

I made up my mind to eat it; the Big Un's share, too, for going off with Nellie. He shouldn't taste a bit, the wretch. The mugs were a study at the first mouthful. Afterwards they pitched in. When I had drunk a half-a-dozen glasses of lemon squash, I felt as though a live eel or two were rowin' inside. I didn't care. I'd eaten his share. Perhaps they thought me greedy when, like Oliver Twist, I asked for more.

Suddenly, at the flutter of a dress, the table was deserted, leaving Tucker, Will and self. When we looked out, there was the Ad' and Jimbly trying which could get nearest the cook. Wilkie was already walking off with another maid, bidding defiance with his arm round her waist. Then I thought of Wilson Blend.

Jimbly apparently deserted his intentions as to the cook, leaving Ad' in sole possession. Wilkie was far away on the cliff, so in the twilight we rambled on, too. Presently we saw him turn round to come back. Then somebody suggested something, whereupon each one rendered up his belt and they were joined together. Now, on the cliff were sundry blackberry bushes and advantage of these were taken, and in the dim light two forms lay down under cover, one each side of the path, with arms extended, stretching the belts across forming a barrier. The rest wandered on to avoid suspicion.

Wilkie and the maid came slowly on, as is the way with swains and maids, gazing heavenwards, oblivious of the snare awaiting them. He was bending over her suspiciously near her face, and the maiden looked away out at sea. I won't swear to anything that happened but it completely upset the gravity of the two holding the belts and made them shake, which caught the other eye of the maiden. Unable to contain themselves further, the belt-bearers gave one awful roar and left. So near. Almost on it. One step more and the carefully planned scheme would have been accomplished. It was vexatious.

Wilkie said strong language when we lay down to sleep that evening. He needn't have done it because it was inconvenient to us as well as himself, being deprived of our only means of suspense for some time.

When we came up to the Ad' and the cook, we were told we must go up to the house, so we went and fetched the crockery, silver and fine linen, and the whole lot trooped up the back entrance giggling and fooling like a lot of schoolboys. Some led the way and we followed. We went through a kitchen and turned into a snug little room. Then Nellie and the Big Un came in looking terrrible silly. The seven chaps arranged themselves as best the furniture would allow, and Ad' sitting sort of chairman-like on a table.

Have you ever been into a gentleman's house in sort of a derogatory manner, in a good number, say half-a-dozen or so, eat his fare and drank his cheer? Because if so, you know the sort of humiliating feeling which comes to one, especially is this the case, when the owner is a man of large physique and enjoys good health.

There was nothing to do. We weren't allowed to smoke, as the major-domo objected. I don't mean we asked him – this information was conveyed to us by the cook when we attempted to light up.

I found a week-old Globe, which was very acceptable. On being asked, "What news?" I read a little Parliamentary news out. From that, we found the cook was a rank radical, which confirmed the suspicion I

Christchurch Priory.

CHRISTCHURCH PRIORY.

had before formed from the equality she carried out in the distribution of her master's goods. She was a bit of a thought-reader in her way and spirit-rapping was not an unknown science to her. Jimbly and others asked for information on the subject, which saved us from a display, for which we are heartily thankful.

Then lemon squash was handed round. It isn't fit drink to give to a pig, but one couldn't find fault, but our pretty tipple of previous nights was missed. The cook sent Big Un and Nellie out for two spoons. I didn't think that right – we should have had two spoons if they had stayed in the room.

The time dragged on slow. We could only sit and look at each other, thinking what bally rot it was. Then Nellie came to the rescue a bit and showed us a painting of herself, executed by her brother, in Greek costume, depicted as a maiden in a cave by the seashore. The lines were rather severe, but there was certainly a likeness. The sea was very green and the sky blue. It isn't for me to criticize, though.

The squash began to work on Jimbly, causing him to fling the chairs about, catch 'old of the maidens in an excited manner, and do other things in which we joined him. Then came a rapping and a message from the Missus for just a little quietness.

"We'd better go."

After shaking hands and farewells, we made shift. Of course, the maidens must see us off the premises. Things occurred here which oughtn't to. There was a loud smack heard and the cook's ruffled voice exclaimed: "Now that's carrying a joke too far." Roars of laughter as we all tumbled one over the other in the dark to find out who it was. The fellow must have been very hard up for a kiss. He's used, perhaps, to have a plentiful supply daily and the loss caused him to forget himself. Certain it's the last kiss the cook will ever have unless it's in the dark, when Shakespeare says "one woman as good as another," but on that we have our doubts. However, we mustn't kiss and tell, so we let it lie.

It was by this time nearly 11 p.m. and we set to work to make snug for the night. After one Scotch, we lay down and talked ourselves off to sleep. This was the last of these kind-hearted damsels. What caused them to behave so liberally to us, and to go out of their way to cook, supply and feed us with victuals, is beyond me. Strangers in a strange land, unknown to any of them. Perhaps they haven't got any male specimens down there. They certainly must have missed us when we went. Sometimes now I catch the Big Un sighing; such long sighs. Then I know they're not forgotten and I sigh to myself: "One touch of sorrow makes the whole world akin." Perhaps in the far distant, if it should so be, we may look back to youth's bright days, when the mind was fresh and all the world seemed good and true; before we had learnt by sad experience all was not what it seemed. Then these days spent in innocent pleasure will stand before us, and "our life was not all sadness" will be the verdict.

Bidding these maids greetings and farewells, we leave them, hoping that our mutual intercourse may be of benefit to us all. Indeed, it has taught us that kindness comes from the least expected and most unthought of quarter.

We awoke refreshed, and prepared the morning meal. It was the sabbath and we were to start on our homeward journey, so we were busy preparing, packing the remainder of provisions, personal effects. Striking tent etc., we handed over the key to the coastguards with a certain remuneration for their kindness, but it was given without any thought of reward. A finer, better-hearted body of men you won't meet than our English coastguards. Long life and happiness to them.

So, after 10, we gave our last long look at the spot where we had spent such happy days. Sorrowing to leave it, we pushed off from the shore. There was a steady breeze and we in the heavier boat started last, up sails. The rippling of the water on the bow was sweet music and the distant sound of the Priory bells was not unappreciated. And when we

"When Blackwater Ferry was come to, the Big Un took a view."
Photo by Arthur Kerridge.

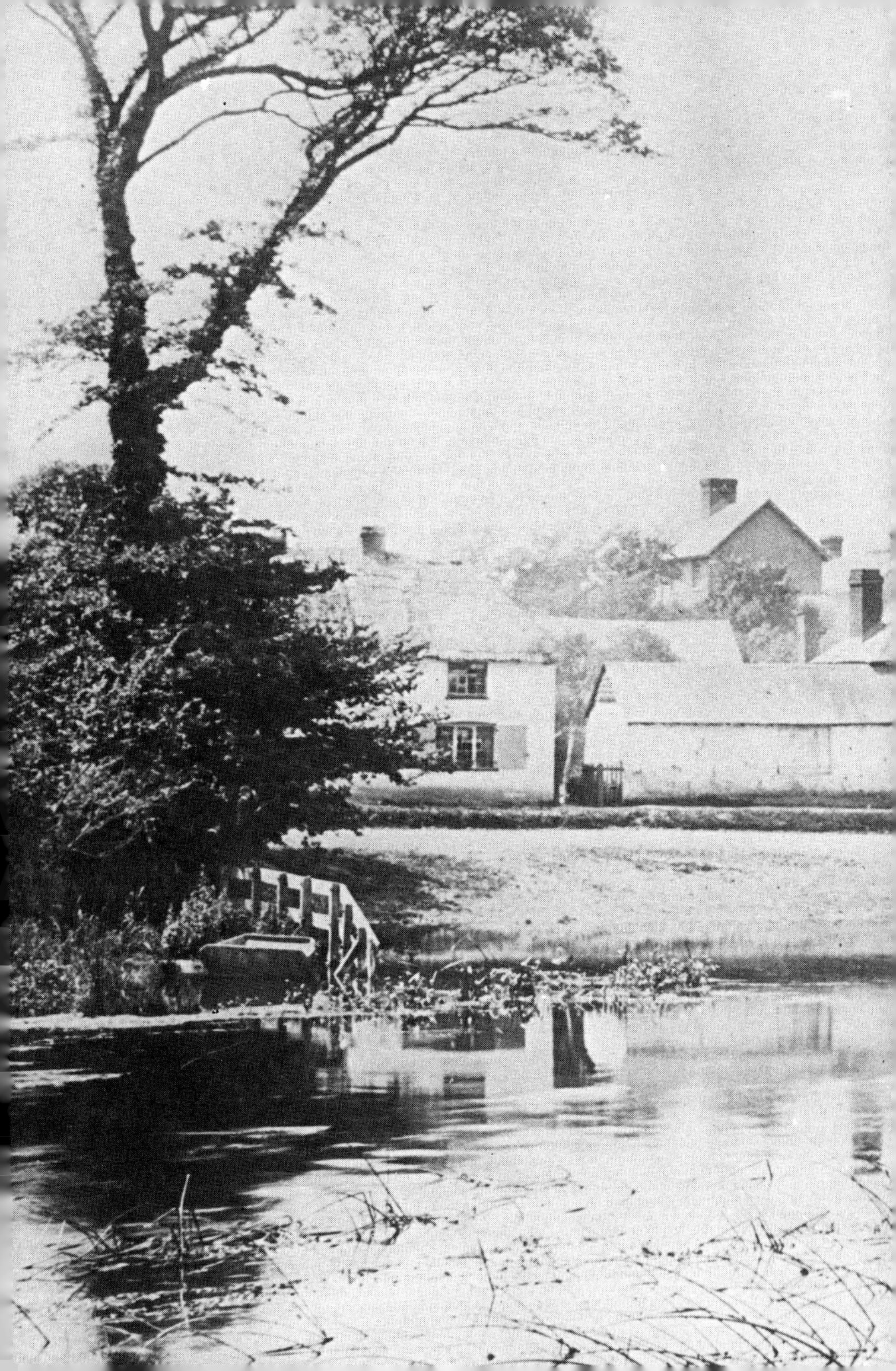

Iford, c. 1900.

Throop Mill today. Photo by Phil Yeomans.

got nearer we could hear the organ pealing forth the familiar strains. Each one intently listened and no-one spoke to mar the spell. Each thought his thunks quietly for once.

We joined the other boat at the quay, set our visitor ashore and bid adieu. We may never meet again but the remembrance, I think, will be lasting.

As the river narrowed, the sails were taken down and we rowed independently. It was hard work against stream and by the time the New Inn, Iford, was reached, it was past noon. Here we lay in a store of biscuits and then settled down to the regular course of one hour on, two off, towing.

The weeds, the weeds! It was the one cry, and to add to further trouble, the river was considerably lower than when we came down. It was all very well when you were off duty – you could watch the expressions on the countenances of the rowers and listen to them calling to their patron saints. It was quite amusing. You would see a fellow shaking his oar, trying to dislodge a weed or two, but they

68

The Stour at Dudsbury today.
Photo by Phil Yeomans.

"Rushes and vegetation stretched from bank to bank."
Photo by Phil Yeomans.

wouldn't come off. So he would simply ignore their existence and row on, until they got so thick that the weight reminded the rower they were still there and at last stopped him. Then he would shut his eyes and pull, determining something shall give, so something generally did. Then there was a row and swearing pretty general. There was some exceptions. You would see some determine to take it quietly, go to a lot of trouble when their oars got weedy, unship them, shake off and gently replace. This was all very well for the first ten minutes – then they joined the majority, swearing in every key from a hiss to deep bass. I've lived through a lot but I never expected to live through that.

When Blackwater Ferry was come to, the Big Un took a view. As he was on rowing, I think it was just a manoeuvre to plank out time.

We came to Throop after much labour and more swearing. Here was a weir. Everybody was bad-tempered and after we had got the light boat across, and were about to launch the heavy one, the owner of the mill came out like one demented and swore by all that's good and bad we shouldn't pass. He might have saved himself the trouble. Swearing we were quite used to of late and we were in a bad mood. We didn't care much what he did. We explained we had got leave from his son and ended the business by purchasing some butter from the old boy.

One more boating expedition, and then if the laws aren't altered as to navigation of rivers, cutting weeds, and free permission to everyone granted, landlords abolished and weirs destroyed, I'll turn radical. The way we were badgered was too awful.

We came to by the side of the river above Throop and, being past 4 p.m., made the water hot and had tea in our impromptu style, eating the food in the boats. When finished, we pushed on, as we intended camping at the same place as when we came down. It was sorrowful work. Stillness reigned on that beautiful Sunday evening, broken only by a muttered curse or a guttural sound which meant the same. Sometimes we had to put a man in the bow of each boat and shove the rushes and weeds on either side to lessen the labour, and the masts were used as poles for propelling. Seven, eight and nine, yet no resting. The moon had risen beautiful and clear, but on the river was a mist and the shadows thrown by the moon looked weird and gruesome. At last, thank goodness, the boats were moored to the bank, tent pitched, a hasty meal composed of lunch biscuits, beef and whisky (provisions has run down to that). With scarce a sound, all lay down and were soon asleep.

It was quite 5 a.m. Monday morning when I awoke or, strictly speaking, was awaken. Everybody looked very black and unkind at me, though why I couldn't think. But the Big Un soon informed me, in language more forcible than polite: "You little sinner. I shouldn't have thought such an insignificant chap could have made such a row."

From what they told me (you can believe it or not), snoring of a most unusual kind was going on. The ordinary snore is caused by people keeping their mouths open when sleeping, but this was not an ordinary snore. It was composed of two distinct sounds, one taking in the air and the other by expelling it. Jimbly called it "snoring 'em in and out". The Admiral became awakened by some means. Thinking it was Kelly, he dropped him one. The snoring went on. Kelly then lays into Will. No abatement. Then into Jimbly. Still it continued. Jimbly being spiteful at being aroused lays it on stiff to the Big Un and still it went on. Then the entire company pitched into me. It gave place to another sound then. Perhaps I did snore – I was very tired. I tried to explain to them what made me snore but they would have none of me. This is partly why I write these few words – to explain why I snored.

Being tired that night, I dropped off to sleep the sleep of the righteous. It was a beautiful sleep, calm and undisturbed up to a certain stage. Then I seemed to be on a broad expanse of water, with the water rippling gently against the boat. I was the sole occupant except a large spider who had the tiller ropes. He wasn't half bad. Told me all about the doings in Spiderland. Asked me to become a spider, which I readily

Canford Mill.

assented to. He told me he was a man once, lived and had his being, died and became a spider. I asked him which was best. He put aside the tiller ropes, ran along the thwart, settled himself on my knee, looked up with his beady eyes and knowing grin: "Which was best, did you say? Ah-ah-ah! No comparison. When I was a man I was being continually pounced on by the other men. For no other reason but that I was poor, I had to do exactly as I was told, and they thrived and grew rich out of my handiwork, my brains, my toil. "Now," said he, slapping me on the back, "I do the pouncing. I grab, I slay, I kill. Oh, I'm a slayer. Is it any wonder I'm a spider? Come and be a spider, too." Signing me to follow, he dropped over the stern and was lost to view.

Now, during this conversation the clouds had gathered black and gloomy and the waters were troubled. Darkness came on. I shipped the oars and began to row. The water hissed and seemed alive. I looked over the gunwale. Just as I put my arm on the rail, it was seized by a long, clinging sucker which caused me to savagely draw it back. And, lo! the water was full of testaceous animals clawing one another and striving one over the other to reach me in the boat, lashing the water with their huge tentacles. It was a sight never to be forgotten. Only the frail boat's timbers between me and the mass of striving, slippery, death-gripping devils; the evil, horrible smile as they jostle one against the other, moving and swaying backwards and forwards with the motion of the water, drove me mad.

Clutching one of the oars, I mounted the middle thwart and smote at them. But when the oar touched the water, hundreds of gloating tentacles seized it and, with difficulty, I could only raise it. One huge monster, with his green suckers, refused to leave go, hanging on to the struggling mass of devils with his clingers and the oar with other suckers, making a moaning, hissing sound. He was pulling hard. Other outstretched arms strived to reach his achievement, climbing up his huge body to reach the oar.

The boat was going over by reason of the weight and the pulling of other devils. It was one mass of death-dealing hell-hounds, visiting me in the form of jellyfish of every kind, octopus, pholades, cuttlefish, nautilus, with here and there a crustaceous specimen, whose shells grated roughly and were even smashed by the violence as they heaped one on the other, clawing, fighting and struggling. The sight was loathsome in the extreme. Could I be changed to Charon; am I indeed the ferryman of hell? The only response was a louder sound. They seemed to be increasing in thousands: nothing could be seen but a huge, swelling, heaving mass of corruption. One desperate effort I would make. I lashed with the other oar. Then it dawned on me. Why fight?

There's no retreat; there's no advance. Yes, it was true – no escape. I grew giddy and lay down. The thought that I might tumble into the heaving hell sickened me. In despair, I shut my eyes. When I opened them, a huge octopus with his eight arms, which he expanded and contracted as he came along slowly, was making for me. I had nothing to defend myself; oars were gone. I could see the end sticking up now and again as the terrible battle waged. It was death. When once those terrible suckers close on you, they never relax, but the terrible grip grows stronger. The green, shiny body gives. It cannot be torn. They suck the warm, warm, blood. As I sank, I felt his loathsome arms close round my neck.

Was it any wonder I snored? I don't think so. Yet the crew were unkind. If they had dreamt the same dream, perhaps they'd have snored, or even yelled.

Like Pharoah's baker, I wanted the interpretation of the dream when I remembered. The last scene was on the water but the horrible devils had sunk to the level of mere weeds. I had it! It was weeds. They had taken the form proscribed to them in various oaths of yesterday. Moral – don't swear.

"Never was I more glad to see the suspension bridge ..."

*Wimborne railway viaduct, c. 1892. It was demolished in 1978.
Photo by Skipper Brett.*

We were up soon after 6 a.m. Monday morning and started off without any breakfast, as provisions had run out except a tin of beef and some biscuits, which two gents appropriated to themselves. We were all eager for home. The morning was cold as November and threatened with rain. It was reeds and rapids, the same old curse.

We got to Longham, pulled out and got over the rolling bay. We sat in the boats and really shivered. The rushes and vegetation stretched from bank to bank. Frequently we had to come back when halfway through and try another route. The children of Israel never cursed their luck more than we did. Everybody worked, either with oars, poles or tongue. No food, not a bit or drop to cheer up a chap. A fellow can't look happy when he's nothing in his hold. To have something there, we stowed our gas.

Just below Canford, where the river was about a few feet wide, a tree had fallen across. If it took us a second, it took us half-an-hour to get by, and this was not accomplished until severe damage was done to our persons. The Ad' had the mast, shoving with all his might. I had an oar, Wilkie another.

"Now then, all together."

The mast knocks Will in the eye, me in the stomach, Wilkie everywhere. There was confusion for some time after but we got by somehow. Then as far as Canford House, where we had to wade. Then into the deep pool by the rolling bay, and another removal by the overland route, the last and worst, but it was home sweet home when we got over this. No-one seemed to care. It was home sweet home and friends to greet us there. Ahm! all over the place. You couldn't stop 'em from shouting it. We gave a hearty salvo to the enquiry of the miller at the mill if we had got back. Never was I more glad to see the suspension bridge and the viaduct and the others shared with me. We got to the landing place and touched the river bank, not to wander again that year.

We selected our personal belongings and valuables, leaving the other things to be fetched, and made for our respected homes. We were a good bit bronzed, in the best of health and sweetest of tempers.
"See you tonight, I s'pose?" somebody asked for a joke.
"And you too?"
"Ah, I can't tonight. I've got an engagement."
"So've I," says the other.
We understood with a laugh.
The people came to the doors; apprentice boys looked through the windows; small dogs followed behind, all viewing the now-famed travellers.
We hung up at the small shop, where the expedition was first planned, for some time, until the pressure of people became so great as to endanger the lives of the people within.
After, we separated, one to his farm, another to his merchandise, and thus ended the most pleasant holiday it has been my lot to spend.

Many a pleasant chat and pipe we had discussing the incidents. Each time a fresh yarn is appended.
"I say, we ought to have a written account and keep as a memento."
They all chimed in.
"Yes, Skipper, you're the quill driver."
After many days, here's the result – a confused jumble of statements. I don't pretend to be a writer or historian and my advice to anyone who reads it and doesn't like it is to do the other thing. It isn't wanted to be liked. I say the same as a well-known poet:
Some write a neighbour's name to lash,
Some write vain thoughts for idle cash;
But I – an aim I never fash!

    I write for fun.

March 16th 1893

EJB

Many a pleasant chat and pipe we had discussing the incidents, each time a fresh yarn's appended; I say we ought to have a written account and keep as a memento, They all chim'ed in 'Yes, Skipper your the quill driver,' After many days, here's the result a confused jumble of statements, I dont pretend to be a writer or historian and my advise to any one who reads it and dosent like it is to do the other Thing, it is'nt wanted to be like'd, I say the same as a well known poet.

Some write a neighbour's name to lash!
Some write vain thoughts for idle cash;
But I — an aim I never fash!
    I write for Fun.

March 16th
1893
EB

Final page of Brett's manuscript.

IN LOVING MEMORY OF

HENRY EDWARD LANGER,
THE DEARLY LOVED (SECOND) SON OF
HENRY, & ELIZABETH LANGER,
ACCIDENTALLY DROWNED
IN THE RIVER STOUR, ON
SATURDAY JULY 15TH 1893,
AGED 20 YEARS.

"WHAT I DO THOU KNOWEST NOT NOW;
BUT THOU SHALT KNOW HEREAFTER."
JOHN XIII, 7.
"THOU KNOWEST NOT, FOR HERE WE SEE BUT DARKLY
THE OUTLINES OF HIS GRACE;
THE REST IS LEARNT IN HEAVENS ETERNAL GLORY,
AND FACE TO FACE".

THIS STONE WAS ERECTED AS A TOKEN
OF AFFECTION AND ESTEEM BY FRIENDS
CONNECTED WITH THE CONGREGATIONAL
CHURCH OF THIS TOWN.

A tragic postscript from Brett's album. Harry Langer drowned after a canoe capsized on the Stour at Wimborne in 1893. A local paper reported that "Langer gallantly exerted himself to save his friend Ralph Elcock and lost his own life in the attempt. Elcock was rescued." Beneath his photograph of the memorial stone, Skipper Brett wrote the poignant comment: "So ends all things."

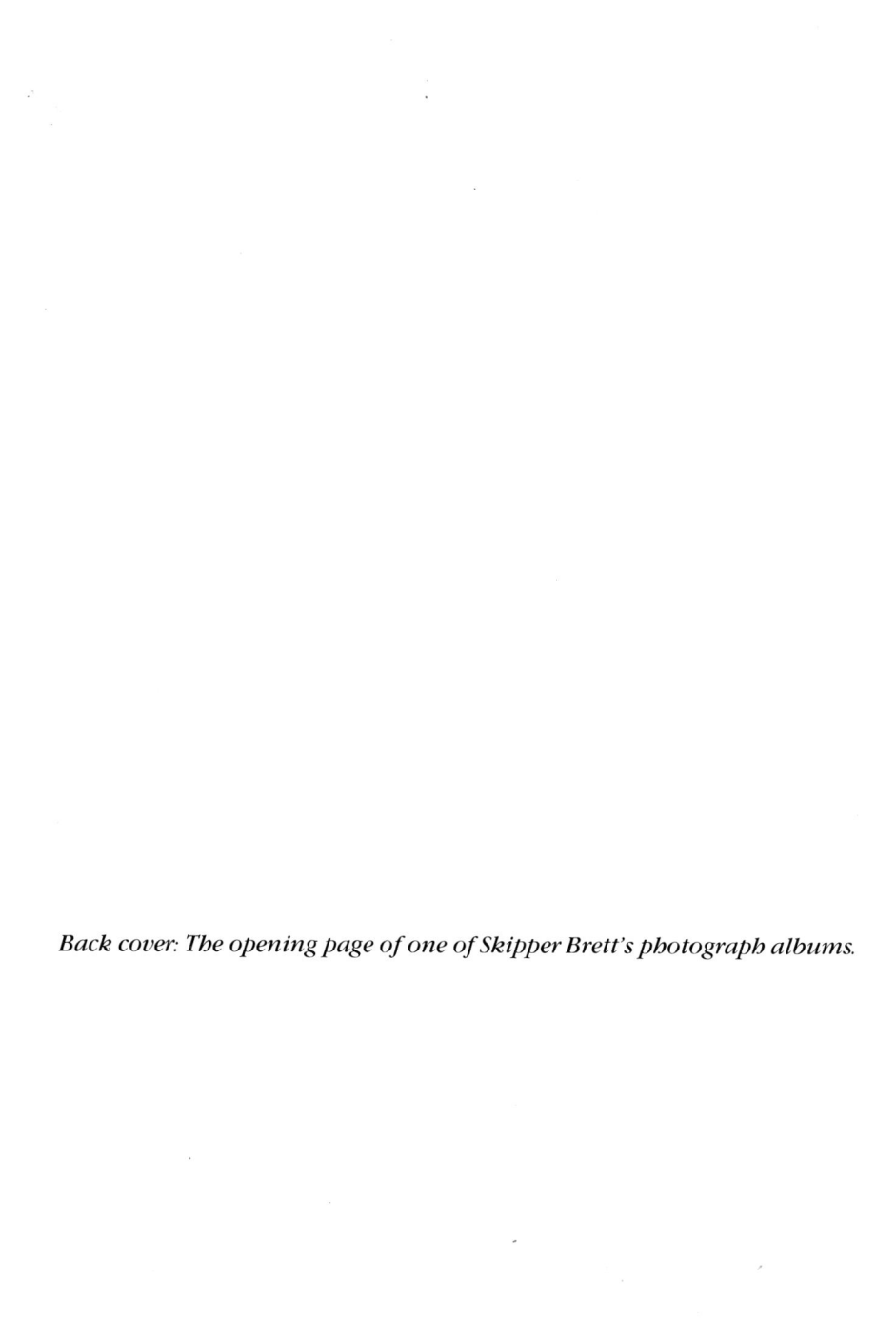

Back cover: The opening page of one of Skipper Brett's photograph albums.